QUILT
YOURSELF GORGEOUS

24 irresistible fat quarter quilts and homestyle projects

Mandy Shaw

David and Charles

This book is dedicated to my mum
Joanie, lost in her own world

A DAVID & CHARLES BOOK
Copyright © David & Charles Limited 2008

David & Charles is an F+W Publications Inc. company
4700 East Galbraith Road,
Cincinnati, OH 45236

First published in the UK in 2008
First published in the US in 2008

Text and designs copyright © Mandy Shaw 2008
Photography and Illustrations copyright © David and Charles 2008

The author and publisher have made every effort to ensure that all the
instructions in the book are accurate and safe, and therefore cannot
accept liability for any resulting injury, damage or loss to persons or
property, however it may arise.

Names of manufacturers, fabric and thread ranges and other products
are provided for the information of readers, with no intention to infringe
copyright or trademarks.

A catalogue record for this book is available from the British Library.

ISBN-13: 978-0-7153-2825-5 hardback
ISBN-10: 0-7153-2825-5 hardback

ISBN-13: 978-0-7153-2830-9 paperback
ISBN-10: 0-7153-2830-1 paperback

Printed in China by SNP Leefung
for David & Charles
Brunel House, Newton Abbot, Devon

Commissioning Editor: Jane Trollope
Desk Editor: Demelza Hookway
Project Editor: Lin Clements
Senior Designer: Sarah Clark
Production Controller: Ros Napper
Photographers: Kim Sayer and Karl Adamson

Visit our website at www.davidandcharles.co.uk
David & Charles books are available from all good bookshops;
alternatively you can contact our Orderline on 0870 9908222 or write
to us at FREEPOST EX2 110, D&C Direct, Newton Abbot, TQ12 4ZZ
(no stamp required UK only); US customers call 800-289-0963 and
Canadian customers call 800-840-5220.

Contents

Introduction

Welcome to my world of sewing: I am a maker of all things lovely! Creating beautiful things has always been part of my life. My earliest memories are of my mum sitting at her knitting and sewing machines making me dolls and their clothes. I used to just sit and watch, happy to quietly hand over the pins. It was often bedtime before the doll was finished but when I woke in the morning the doll would be sitting at the end of my bed. Fortunately, I took after my mum and nearly 40 years on I still have that all-consuming passion for making things.

I spent my early years indulging in crocheting, knitting, macramé and sewing. I created everything from the fabulous to the obscure (including a patchwork bath hat!). I should have been dancing the night away, but I just kept sewing. I had a very traditional sewing teacher, Miss Swift, who noticed that I was keen and talented. She nurtured me, even taking me to Liberty of London to buy fabric and then afterwards for tea at Fortnum and Mason. Reward indeed! Searching my ancestors, hoping to find, perhaps, a skilled Court seamstress I discovered that my great, great grandmother was a coffin liner!

Creating homely items with fabric has continued to be a vital part of my life and I feel strongly that we should share our skills with the next generation, just as the past generation did with me.

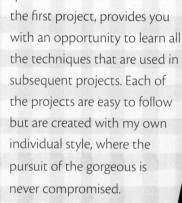

Creating something special from whatever I can lay my hands on has been central to my whole life. My family, three gorgeous girls and my lovely son, have been on the receiving end of all of my endeavours – from dolls, teddies and pirates, to dresses, birthday bunting and quilts. My wonderful husband Phil, a joiner, and I have provided a home brimming with handmade treasures. I want to share some of my magic with you so that your home can be adorned with those special items that make a house a home.

I take my influences from the important events that all families hang their experiences on – birthdays, summer picnics, family weddings, new babies and, of course, the tradition of Christmas. I have to admit I am not a perfectionist. I like quick and fast techniques; I cut corners but not charm, compromising on rules but not on results. I think we have one life to live and we should get on with it! Love what you make, to your own self be true and sew, sew, sew!

The projects in this book are designed to provide you with special items that will enhance your world. They have been created to mark an event, an occasion or special circumstance. The Welcome Quilt, the first project, provides you with an opportunity to learn all the techniques that are used in subsequent projects. Each of the projects are easy to follow but are created with my own individual style, where the pursuit of the gorgeous is never compromised.

Welcome Sampler

This is a delightful little sampler wall hanging. I always teach beginners using a small sampler quilt similar to this one: it is quick to make, takes up little room, is easy to quilt and gets finished! Making this quilt as your first project from this book is an excellent idea as most of the techniques used in this sampler will appear again in the other projects, so you will become familiar with them very quickly.

I made my daughters one each when they left their junior school and asked their teachers and friends to sign the back. It's something they will treasure forever. I also wrote the school motto (by Henry Van Dyke) on the back of their quilts:

Use what talents you possess; the woods would be very silent
if no birds sang there except those that sang the best.

Quilt shows too would be very dull if only the very best quilts were exhibited; I think a lot of quilters would give up and start another hobby if we had only the top-notch standard as inspiration. For this quilt I used the fat eighth bundles you buy at quilt shows and never know what to do with, because it uses a little of a lot of different fabrics.

I loved making this sampler quilt because you can learn lots of new skills and improve your techniques without getting bogged down on huge blocks you don't like. You could replace the flying geese with an appliquéd 'welcome' block and then it really will be at home on the wall in your hall.

Welcome Quilt

The fabrics used in this quilt were from a fat eighth bundle bought at a quilt show. They all go well together in colour and tone and I used up nearly every one, especially in the borders. Which is just as well, because I have a theory that once you have used your fabrics it's unlikely you'll want to use them again in the near future, but if you leave them for the future they will then be outdated! Any fabrics you do have left over can be patched together to use as a backing – now that's frugal!

Finished size: 30½in x 24½in (77.5cm x 62.3cm)
Techniques: Making Flying Geese (page 13) ● Using templates (page 96) ● Fusible webbing (page 96) ● Foundation piecing (page 97) ● Appliqué (page 98) ● Using ric-rac (page 99) ● Adding Borders (page 99) ● Layering (page 100) ● Quilting (page 100) ● Binding (page 101) ● Labelling your quilt (page 101)

Ingredients

o A bundle of ten fabrics, each a fat eighth
o One fat quarter of fabric for background (mine's a black fabric with stars)
o Backing fabric 28in x 34in (71.2cm x 86.4cm) (this can be patched from scraps)
o Cotton wadding (batting) 28in x 34in (71.2cm x 86.4cm)
o Fusible webbing
o Sashing ¼yd (0.25m)
o Binding 4yd (4m)
o Ric-rac braid 4yd (4m)
o Ten buttons to decorate
o Matching embroidery thread
o Lightweight sew-in interfacing

Quick Tip . . .
When ironing on the fusible webbing, the smooth side of the iron goes on the smooth side of the sheet and the rough side faces the fabric – otherwise you will glue the heart to the iron!

Making the heart squares

1 Seam allowances throughout are an accurate ¼in (6mm) – this is especially important in this quilt so it all fits neatly together like a jigsaw. The quilt layout is shown in the picture opposite. Begin by cutting four 4½in (11.4cm) squares. Enlarge the heart template from page 104 by 200% on a photocopier and trace it on to the smooth side of your fusible webbing. Cut the shape out roughly, not on the line. Iron the fusible webbing with the heart drawn on, on to the *wrong side* of your chosen fabric (see Tip above). Cut out the heart shape accurately on the line, peel off the backing paper, position the heart in the middle of the square and iron it in place. Join the four squares together using a ¼in (6mm) seam allowance.

Making the sunshine patch

2 From your background fabric cut a rectangle exactly 5½in x 6½in (14cm x 16.5cm). Enlarge the sunshine pattern from page 104 by 200% on a photocopier and trace it on to some lightweight sew-in interfacing. Cut a piece of sunshine fabric 5½in (14cm) square and place this right side to the interfacing. Sew on the *curved line only* of the interfacing, through to the fabric. Trim the curved edge close to the stitching. Turn right way out and then press.

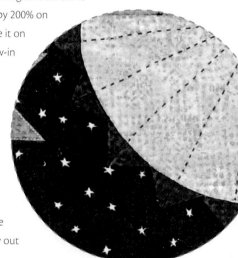

Heart squares

Stars

Sunshine patch

Pieced
Flying Geese

Folded
Flying Geese

Prairie Points

Birdhouse

School

Trees

Pinwheel blocks

Bow Tie blocks

Sashing

Outer border

The layout of the quilt indicating the different blocks, appliquéd areas and ric-rac decoration around the border.

Making the Prairie Points

3 To make the Prairie Points that curve around the sun, follow Fig 1A–D, cutting six rectangles 2in x 1¼in (5.1cm x 3.2cm). Fold over and press ¼in (6mm) at the top of each rectangle and then fold both sides into the middle diagonally and press. Place the sunshine patch in the top right-hand corner of the background fabric rectangle and pin. Tuck the Prairie Points a ¼in (6mm) under the curved edge of the sun, slightly overlapping if necessary. Pin, tack and sew together.

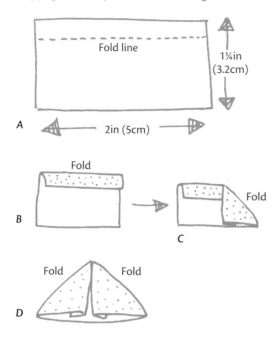

Fig 1 Making the Prairie Points for the sunshine patch (A–D) – make 5 units

Making the folded Flying Geese

4 Cut eight rectangles for the 'geese' 2½in x 1½in (6.3cm x 3.8cm). From the background fabric cut sixteen 1½in (3.8cm) squares. Following Fig 2, fold one rectangle *wrong sides* together and put the folded rectangle on to the right side of one of the squares, matching all raw edges in one corner (A). Place the other square on top, right sides together and sew down one side with a ¼in (6mm) seam, which should incorporate the fold of the rectangle (B). Open out and press the seam open, flattening the little triangle at the top of the seam (C and D). Sew the folded Flying Geese together in a row, using the tip of the triangle as your sewing guide. Note: r.s = right side of fabric; w.s = wrong side.

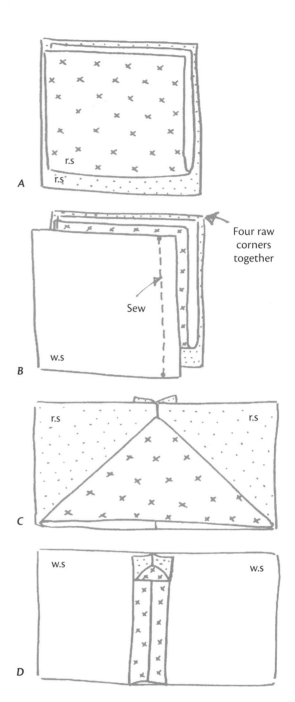

Fig 2 Making the folded Flying Geese (A–D) – make 8 units

Making the stars

5 Cut a 2½in (6.3cm) square for the centre of the star. Cut eight 1½in (3.8cm) squares in the same colour as the centre squares. Cut four rectangles 2½in x 1½in (6.3cm x 3.8cm) in the background colour.

6 On the wrong side of all of the squares draw a line across diagonally (A on Fig 3). Place a square on to the rectangle, right sides together, corners matching and sew on the marked line accurately (B). Cut off the corner and press the triangle back (C). Repeat with another square and the other corner of the rectangle. Do this to the other three rectangles.

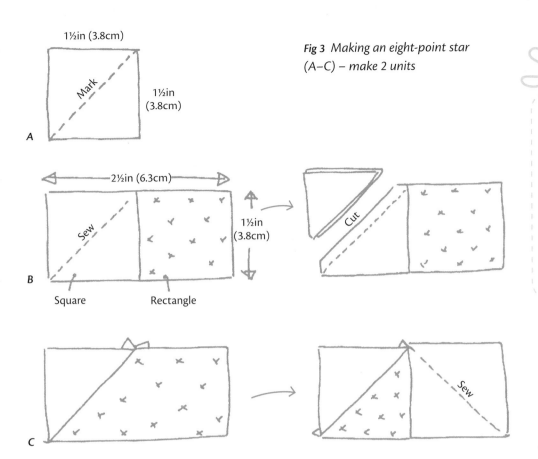

1½in (3.8cm)

Mark

1½in (3.8cm)

A

Fig 3 *Making an eight-point star (A–C) – make 2 units*

2½in (6.3cm)

Sew

1½in (3.8cm)

Cut

B

Square   Rectangle

Sew

C

Quick Tip. . .
After saving scraps all my life, I've had to accept that I can't possibly use them all up, so now I save them in a bag to give to the local play group – the scraps are just the right size for the children to use when making collages.

7 Cut four 1½in (3.8cm) squares of background fabric and construct the star in three rows (Fig 4 below).

Background square + a pieced rectangle + background square (A).
Pieced rectangle + large centre square + pieced rectangle (B).
Background square + a pieced rectangle + background square.
Now sew these three rows together.

8 Make another star block. Press, check sizes and adjust if necessary and then sew the two stars together. Now sew the folded flying geese strip to the bottom of the stars. On the right of these blocks sew the sunshine patch. Open out all seams and press.

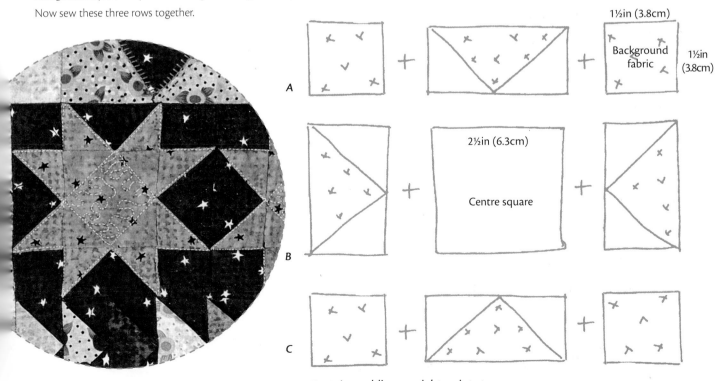

1½in (3.8cm)

Background fabric

1½in (3.8cm)

A

+   +

2½in (6.3cm)

Centre square

B

+   +

C

+   +

Fig 4 *Assembling an eight-point star*

Making the birdhouse

9 From sky background fabric, cut a rectangle 3½in x 5½in (8.9cm x 14cm). From green fabric cut a rectangle 3½in x 2½in (8.9cm x 6.3cm). Sew these two rectangles together with a ¼in (6mm) seam for the birdhouse block. Enlarge the templates on page 104 by 200% and use to cut out the shape. Use blanket stitch (see page 102) to appliqué the birdhouse on to the fabric.

Making the trees

10 The trees in this quilt are foundation pieced (see page 97), which is a technique where fabric patches are stitched to the reverse of a foundation fabric. Begin by enlarging the tree templates on page 104 by 200% on a photocopier and printing twice on to cheap paper (this is easier to sew through than expensive, heavier papers).

Quick Tip. . .

Foundation piecing can be confusing, much like trying to pat your head and rub your tummy at the same time, but persevere, because once mastered the advantages are great and you will be able do complicated blocks and angles with precision and ease – see also page 97.

11 Cut out one paper foundation pattern roughly ¼in (6mm) from the marked *outside* line. Using the second paper foundation pattern, cut out all the shapes on the *inside* line. These will be used as cutting out templates for each pattern piece. Take pattern piece 1, place it on to the wrong side of a piece of trunk fabric, with the right side of the pattern piece up. Pin in place and cut out with a *generous* ½in (1.3cm) seam – this is very important – don't be mean with fabric unless you are experienced with foundation piecing. Pin this piece of fabric on to the wrong side of the trunk template, making sure you cover the whole trunk shape. You will not be able to see the shape so you may have to hold it up to the light. Pin in place.

12 Take pattern piece 2, place it on to the wrong side of a piece of green fabric making sure the right side of the pattern piece is facing you. Pin in place and cut out with a generous ½in (1.3cm) seam. Place this piece of fabric, right sides together on to the trunk, on the side where it will cover shape 2. Pin along the line between 1 and 2, and flip it back to check it will cover shape 2 (hold it up to the light). If all is well, re-adjust your pins so you can sew over them. Turn the fabric and pattern over and sew on the line between 1 and 2 – this will be on the right side of the paper where the pattern is marked and may feel wrong, but I promise you it's right! Flip back to check all is still well and that all the pattern, including outside seam allowances, are covered. Trim the seam allowance to a rough ¼in (6mm) and press.

13 Repeat this procedure with pattern piece number 3. Pattern piece number 4 is the tree and 5 and 6 are background fabric. Once the block is sewn trim it to the correct size, i.e., the *outside* line of the seam allowance. Do not remove the paper until the blocks are sewn together – this will protect any bias edges and help keep them nice and square. When you have made the two trees join them together, using the seam allowance on the papers. Leave the foundation paper in place for the moment.

Making the school

14 *Roof:* the roof is foundation pieced – enlarge the roof pattern on page 104 by 200% and follow the technique described for the trees above. Be aware that the roof template is in reverse. Cut two background rectangles one 2½in x 1½in (6.3cm x 3.8cm) and another 3½in x 1½in (8.9cm x 3.8cm). Cut a piece for the chimney 1½in (3.8cm) square. Join the shorter strip to the left side of the chimney and the longer to the right side. Sew this to the top of the roof. Leave the foundation paper in place for the moment.

15 *Door:* cut three rectangles 1½in x 2½in (3.8cm x 6.3cm), two in house colour and one in door colour. Cut another rectangle 3½in x 1½in (8.9cm x 3.8cm) also in house colour. Using ¼in (6mm) seams, sew these rectangles together, two shorter house ones either side of the door and the longer one across the top (see Fig 5 below).

16 *Window:* cut three 1½in (3.8cm) squares, two in house colour and one in window colour. Cut two rectangles 3½in x 1½in (8.9cm x 3.8cm) also in house colour. Using ¼in (6mm) seams, sew the two house squares either side of the window square and then sew a rectangle to the top and bottom of the squares.

17 Assemble the school by first sewing the two pieced squares together (window and door). Sew these to the bottom of the roof. Sew the trees to the right of the house and the appliquéd birdhouse to the left of the house. Appliqué the circular window in place above the door and edge with blanket stitch (see the picture detail in the circle, below left). Now sew these blocks to the bottom of the stars/flying geese/sunshine block.

Making the pieced Flying Geese

18 Make the larger flying geese using the foundation paper pattern on page 104 and the technique described for the trees opposite. Enlarge the pattern by 200% and print twice to get the required numbers of flying geese. Keep the foundation paper in place until the sashing has been sewn on.

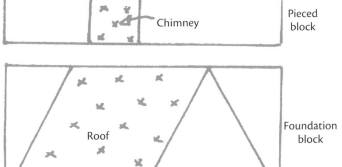

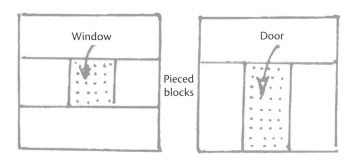

Fig 5 *Assembling the house patches*

19 Sew the flying geese to the left side of the house and its blocks. Sew the hearts to the top of the house and its blocks. You are now ready to move on to the Pinwheel blocks.

Quick Tip. . .
When making quilts, especially samplers, I always try to use as many fabrics as possible to make the quilt 'sing'. In this quilt there are at least five different 'lights' for the background – it would look quite dull if I had only used one.

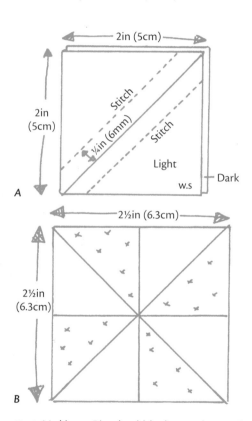

Making the Pinwheel blocks

20 The five Pinwheel blocks are made using a fast and accurate method that you may not be familiar with. Cut a *rough* rectangle 3in x 5in (7.6cm x 12.7cm), one from flower fabric and one from background fabric. Iron these two, right sides together. On the lighter side of the fabric mark two exact 2in (5cm) squares, using a fine propelling pencil. Draw in the sewing lines as on Fig 6 below (A). Pin the fabrics together in each half square. With small running stitches, sew along the stitching lines, casting on and off within the squares if sewing by hand, but sewing off the edge if by machine. Using rotary cutters or sharp, long scissors, cut the outside squares first, then the diagonals. Press to set the stitch, then open out your squares and press (don't over press). Re-cut these squares to 1½in (3.8cm).

Fig 6 Making a Pinwheel block – make 5 units

21 Arrange your half-square triangles into a pinwheel as in diagram 6B and sew them together with ¼in (6mm) seams. From garden-themed fabric cut a rectangle 3½in x 2½in (8.9cm x 6.3cm). Sew three pinwheels together, then sew the garden rectangle to the right of these, and then the remaining two pinwheels. Press seams open. Sew a garden strip 13½in x 1½in (34.3cm x 3.8cm) to the bottom of the pinwheels. Sew these strips to the bottom of the houses. Tear off the foundation paper from the house and trees and press seams.

Making the Bow Tie blocks

22 These will appear tricky at first and it may take a few attempts to get it right but when you do it's like magic and will stay with you forever. Follow the eight-part diagram (Fig 7). Cut sixteen 1½in (3.8cm) squares in background fabric. Cut twenty-four 1½in (3.8cm) squares in bow tie fabric. For each bow tie you will need two background and three bow tie squares. Take one bow tie square and fold it in half wrong sides together, place it on top of another bow tie square, all raw edges matching. On top of these squares place a background square, right sides together. Sew down the right side (the side with the folded edge in), but *start* ¼in (6mm) down from the top edge (see 7B).

23 This step is most important. Open out the squares and take point 'b' and place it right into the middle of point 'c'. The reason we have not sewn right to the end of the seam is so that we can get point 'b' right into the corner. Place a bow tie square on top of the folded square, making sure it goes right into the corner – the folded square will now lay on to the right-hand background square. Sew, starting ¼in (6mm) down from the top as before. Open these squares out, and put point 'a' on to point 'c'. This folded square will lie on to the right-hand side square. Place a background square on top and sew, starting ¼in (6mm) down from the top. The final seam is folded together and sewn with no insertions, normally just folding in place.

24 Open the block out, be amazed and press. Press from the back, put the tip of the iron into the middle of all the seams and press them all in a clockwise direction, so they all lay flat. Make seven more Bow Tie blocks. Sew the eight bow ties together and sew the row to the bottom of the house and its blocks and then press.

Sashing

25 Cut four strips of sashing, two 16½in x 1½in (42cm x 3.8cm) and two 24½in x 1½in (62.3cm x 3.8cm). Sew the two shorter strips to the top and bottom of the quilt and press. Sew the two longer strips to the sides of the quilt and press.

Border

26 Cut up all your darker or stronger-coloured fabric into 3½in (8.9cm) wide pieces and join them together quite randomly into two lengths of 18½in (47cm) and two of 30½in (77.5cm). Join the shorter two to the top and bottom of the quilt and the longer two to each side. Press the quilt. This border will be decorated with ric-rac at the quilting stage (step 28).

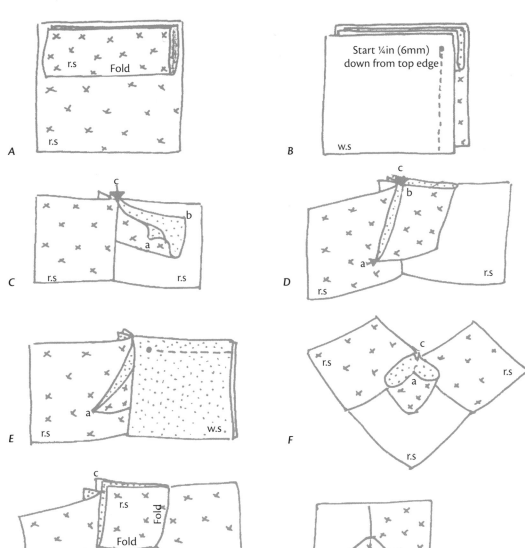

A

B — Start ¼in (6mm) down from top edge — w.s

C — r.s — c — b — a — r.s

D — c — b — a — r.s — r.s

E — a — r.s — w.s

F — c — a — r.s — r.s — r.s

G — c — r.s — Fold — Fold — Fold — r.s — r.s — r.s

H

Fig 7 Making the Bow Tie blocks (A–H) – make 8 units

Layering the quilt

27 Layering means putting the quilt top, wadding and backing together in a 'quilt sandwich', ready for quilting and finishing (see page 100). Prepare the quilt for layering by pressing seams and cutting off stray threads. Cut backing fabric and cotton wadding each 28in x 34in (71.2cm x 86.4cm). Lay the backing fabric on a flat surface, wrong side up and smooth it out. Secure flat with some adhesive tape or masking tape. Lay the wadding on top and smooth it out flat. Place the quilt on top, right side up, smooth it out and pin with safety pins every 3in (7.6cm).

Quick Tip. . .
On smaller projects I sometimes use spray adhesive to fix the layers together. Follow the manufacturer's instructions and wash the quilt once the project is finished.

Quilting and binding

28 Quilt by machine or hand, around the inside of the borders and each block and shape. I decorated the quilt by sewing buttons in the centres of the pinwheels so they looked like flowers, and also on the birdhouse, the school door and the hearts. I sewed rays of 'light' on the sun and ric-rac on the house to give it definition. Just add embellishments wherever you like and have some fun. Finish the quilt by binding with a 2¾in (7cm) wide double binding – see instructions on page 101. Finally, add a label on the back of the quilt with your name, when you made it and why (see page 101).

Spring Chickens

I love all the seasons in Britain but spring comes as such a welcome relief after the highs of Christmas and the lows of dreary January and February. Everyone comes out of hibernation in tune with nature, and those gorgeous green and yellow spring colours, with blue skies and pink blossom on the way, are enough to cheer anyone up.

In our family, spring and Easter are our first celebrations of the year. At home we make Easter trees laden with handmade eggs. Then there is a corny-clued Easter egg hunt, a vain attempt to eat up all the simnel cake and the over-indulged feel of too much chocolate...

My family is growing only too fast and flying my well-lined nest, but I continue to decorate and make it welcoming for them and have added to my collection with this cute running chicken tablemat. If you haven't tried foundation piecing yet, this tablemat is the perfect project. There's also a plump chicken doorstop called Clarence, who is great fun to make. I feel slightly worried about having him as a doorstop on the floor, as our dog Ted hasn't taken his eyes off him yet!

Some foundation piecing and some simple appliqué will welcome spring into your home with this fun tablemat. If you think Clarence is too nice to use as a doorstop, then make him a mate and use them as bookends instead.

Running Chickens Tablemat

This cute tablemat is a welcoming sight in the centre of a table with a lovely vase of spring flowers or a simnel cake on. It's easy to make once you have mastered the foundation-pieced chickens and really takes no time at all.

Finished size: 12in (30.5cm) diameter
Techniques: Using templates (page 96) • Foundation piecing (page 97) • Appliqué (page 98) • Ric-rac (page 99) • Lazy daisy stitch (page 103)

Ingredients

- Fat quarter of main fabric
- Two contrasting fabrics for the chickens 9in x 10in (23cm x 24.5cm) (fat eighth) of each
- Felt 8in (20.3cm) square
- Light sew-in interfacing 10in (25.4cm) square
- Backing fabric 14in (35.5cm) square
- Cotton wadding (batting) 14in (35.5cm) square
- Ric-rac braid ½in (1.3cm) wide x 40in (101.5cm) long
- Skein of embroidery thread to match
- Twelve tiny buttons for eyes or 5mm beads

Foundation piecing

1 Enlarge all the tablemat patterns on page 105 by 200% on a photocopier. Print four copies of the foundation piecing pattern. Foundation piece the sections following the foundation piecing instructions on page 97. Join all four sections together to make a complete circle.

2 Using the pattern piece for the quarter circle, mark a complete circle on to the sew-in interfacing. Place a square of main fabric beneath the interfacing, right sides together and pin. Sew the two together with a very small stitch on the marked line of the circle. Trim away the excess to a very scant ¼in (6mm). Slit the interfacing and turn the right way out. Using a large knitting needle or a wooden chopstick, ease out the circle shape and then press carefully. Place this circle in the centre on top of the foundation chickens. Pin very well all round the circle and then ladder stitch in place (see page 103).

Appliqué

3 Cut eight petals from felt using the petal pattern. Using one of the 'chicken' fabrics and the flower centre, cut a circle. Place the petal under the circle (see picture below) and appliqué in place using blanket stitch. Using the beak and wing patterns cut twelve beaks and wings from felt and appliqué these on to the chickens.

Assembling the mat

4 Tack the ric-rac to the outside edge of the mat (see page 99) and tack the raw ends together so they will not be seen. Place the quilt top on to the backing fabric, right sides together and sit this on top of the cotton wadding. Sew all the way around through all three layers following the tacking line as a guide and leaving a 3in (7.6cm) gap for turning. Trim the seam to a *scant* ¼in (6mm), turn the right way out and ladder stitch the opening closed. Press well.

5 Quilt neatly around the circle in the middle, the flower and each little wing. Sew on the buttons or beads for eyes. Embroider the legs with backstitch (the pattern is given in Fig 1 below). Finish by adding the head feathers with lazy daisy stitch (see page 103).

Fig 1 Backstitch pattern (actual size) for embroidering the chickens' legs

The layout of the tablemat. You can vary the positions of the chicken's wings a little if you desire.

Clarence Chicken

Instead of a doorstop you could use this fun chicken as a bookend, in which case you'll need to make two. You could also reduce the pattern size and make some baby chickens as well. . . ah!

Finished size: 10in (25cm) tall approx (excluding legs)
Techniques: Using templates (page 96) • Ric-rac (page 99) • Blanket stitch (page 102)

Quick Tip. . .
If you can't find plastic pellets there are substitutes in your local pet store, for example, grit and crushed shells for birds. You can use lentils or rice, but they must be dry baked first to kill off any bugs that might be lurking.

1 Enlarge all the patterns on page 105 by 200% on a photocopier. Fold the fat quarter of fabric for the chicken in half, right sides together. Using the body pattern and the folded fabric cut out one body (this automatically creates one in reverse). From a contrasting fabric cut out the tail pattern twice. On folded fabric (to automatically create one in reverse), cut two pairs of wings.

Legs

2 Cut out the leg template on the marked line. Fold your leg fabric right sides together, lengthways, and pin the template to the fabric. *Do not cut* but trace around the template with a pencil. Repeat using the same template, leaving ½in (1.3cm) gap between each leg. Using a smaller than normal stitch, sew on this marked line through both layers of fabric, leaving the top end open. Cut out both legs with a neat, scant ¼in (6mm). Turn the right way out by pushing a pencil with a rubber on the end into the foot of the leg (the rubber acts as a grip). Very lightly stuff the two legs, stopping 2in (5cm) from the top.

Tail

3 Using one tail piece, tack ric-rac braid along the curved edge (see page 99). Place the two tail pieces right sides together and sew on the curved tacked line. Trim this seam, turn right way out and press. Top stitch the curved edge – see Fig 1 below. Now gather the straight edge with a large running stitch.

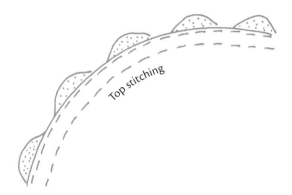

Fig 1 *Top stitching the tail once the ric-rac is in place*

Body

4 Using a smaller stitch than normal, sew the two bodies together leaving openings where indicated on the pattern. On the bottom of the body you have two unsewn square corners. Squash each corner separately 'A' to 'B' and pin (see Fig 2 below and the body template).

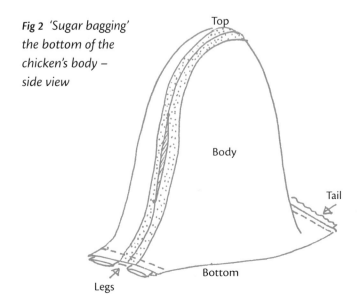

Fig 2 *'Sugar bagging' the bottom of the chicken's body – side view*

5 Pop the two legs in via the opening in the back of the body and poke the ends out of the squashed corner on the front (remove the pins first) – see Fig 3. Make sure they sit side by side and protrude only by a ¼in (6mm). Pin and then sew twice for reinforcement. Do the same with the gathered tail, popping the gathered end into the back opening and poking it out on the back corner by only ¼in (6mm). Pin and sew well. Turn the right way out through the opening. Fill the bottom half of the body with plastic pellets or fine grit, and then stuff the rest really firmly with stuffing. Close the opening with ladder stitch (see page 103).

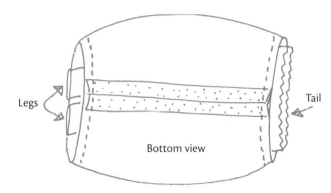

Fig 3 *The legs and tail placed inside the body cavity, as seen from below*

Wings

6 Sew all the way around on both sets of wings. Cut a slit in one layer and turn the right way out. Gently stuff the wings and ladder stitch the opening closed. Blanket stitch (see page 102) all the way around the wings. They can be glued or sewn to the body in the position shown on the pattern.

Comb, beak and wattle

7 Cut out the template for the comb, beak and wattle. Pin it well on to two layers of felt and trace around the outside of the shape. Mark 'A' and 'B': *do not cut out* but sew with a small stitch on the marked line between A and B. Cut out the remainder of the comb, beak and wattle on the marked line and also close to the stitching line. Turn the right way out and stuff gently, especially the wattle. Blanket stitch around the piece, leaving the area between A and B free. Pin points A and B to the body, as indicated on the pattern, tuck under a ¼in (6mm) and ladder stitch each side in position.

8 Sew on two buttons for eyes, taking the stitch through the head to the other eye, so the eyes are indented. Appliqué on a little felt heart. To finish, cut the 12in (30.5cm) square of fabric for the scarf in half diagonally, fray the edges and tie around Clarence's neck.

Baby, Baby

There is nothing in the world lovelier than the smell and sound of a new baby. I think they are delightful – all that wonderful cuddling and snuggling. And what nicer way to do it than with the baby wrapped in a fresh, warm quilt?

For this quilt I deliberately steered clear of bright trendy fabrics and aimed for a timeless French feel. I have chosen an easy nine-patch block with an embroidered alphabet plus an adult bear cuddling a baby bear for the central panel.

Instead of the traditional three layers I just used the quilt top and a very soft fleece called minkie for the backing, which is incredible snugly and quilts really well. With a fast strip-piecing technique and a nice combination of hand and machine quilting you will have this gorgeous quilt made in no time.

This delicately coloured quilt in off-white and pale blue is really easy to make and would make a wonderful gift to some proud parents. There are also two darling teddy bears to accompany the quilt – see instructions on page 27.

Rock-a-bye Baby Quilt

The colour scheme for this lovely quilt can be changed in an instant to pink and off-white or yellow, or whatever else you prefer. I used a ribbon tape to edge the central rectangle and around the edge of the quilt because I just loved the decorative effect it produced but you could bind the quilt in the conventional manner if you prefer.

Finished size: 50in x 44in (127cm x 111.7cm)

Techniques: Using templates (page 96) • Fusible webbing (page 96) • Appliqué (page 98) • Adding borders (page 99) • Layering (page 100) • Binding (page 101)

Ingredients

o   Off-white linen 2yd (2m)

o   Light blue seersucker gingham ¾yd (0.75m)

o   Decorative tape or ribbon ⅝in (1.6cm) wide x 7yd (6.5m)

o   Decorative tape or ribbon ½in (1.3in) wide x 5yd (4.75m), or ⅝in (1.6cm) wide if you prefer

o   Fusible webbing ¼yd (0.25m)

o   Minkie (plush pile fabric) or fleece for backing 1½yd (1.5m)

o   Two skeins of matching embroidery thread

1 From the off-white fabric cut three 6½in (16.5cm) strips across the fabric, from selvage to selvage. From these strips cut eighteen 6½in (16.5cm) squares. Cut a white rectangle 12½in x 18½in (31.8cm x 47cm). Cut four white strips 2½in wide (6.3cm). Cut five blue strips 2½in (6.3cm) wide. Cut five white strips for the borders 2½in (6.3cm) wide and put these to one side.

Appliquéing the teddies

2 Enlarge the templates on page 106 by 200% on a photocopier. Using fusible webbing, trace the body, head, legs and baby bear parts on to the smooth side of the webbing. Cut the shapes out roughly, not on the line. Iron the fusible webbing with the shapes, on to the *wrong side* of your chosen fabric (see the Quick Tip on page 8). Cut out the shapes accurately on the line. On the large bear's body cut into the arms on the red line. Peel off the backing paper. Position the bears in the middle of the rectangle, using the detail picture above as a guide (the large bear's arms can be lifted up so you can snuggle the baby bear in position). Iron in place. Blanket stitch (see page 102) around the edges of the teddies, or use a machine satin stitch for extra definition.

Making the nine-patch blocks

3 Take two blue strips and one white one and sew them together carefully with a ¼in (6mm) seam allowance. The white strip must be in the middle. Press the seams to the middle. Repeat with three more strips. Now take two white strips and one blue and sew them together with a ¼in (6mm) seam allowance. The blue one will be in the middle this time. Press the seam away from the middle this time. Very carefully cut up the sewn strips into 2½in (6.3cm) sections.

4 Sew three of the sewn strips together – two of the predominately blue ones to a predominately white one – the white one will be in the middle (see Fig 1A). Butt up the seam allowances (Fig 1B). Repeat this eighteen times. Be careful that you remain accurate, because then all will fit together well.

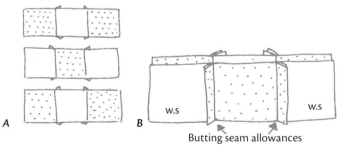

A   B   w.s   w.s

Butting seam allowances

Fig 1 *Assembling a nine-patch block*

5 Enlarge the alphabet and numbers templates from pages 106–107 by 200% on a photocopier and trace the templates. You could include the name and birth date of the baby. These will be embroidered later with backstitch and this will also act as quilting. Enlarge and trace the heart patterns from page 106.

Border

Nine-patch block

abc

def

ghi

jkl

abcdefghij
klmnoperstu
vw xyz

mno

pqr

0123456789

Central Panel

stu

vwx

yz

The layout of the quilt – essentially just a central panel
surrounded by nine-patch blocks and plain, quilted squares.

Using nine of the 6½in (16.5cm) squares, trace on the heart pattern and then trace the large letters on the rest of the squares. These will be embroidered later and act as quilting. Use a very fine and sharp propelling pencil to do the marking. Sew the blocks together as follows, referring to Fig 2.

Row 1: heart block + nine patch + 'abc' block + nine patch + heart block + nine patch.

Row 2: nine patch + heart block + nine patch + 'def' block + nine patch + heart block.

Row 3 (left side): 'ghi' block + nine patch.

Row 4 (left side): nine patch + 'mno' block.

Row 5 (left side): heart block + nine patch.

Sew the left-hand side rows 3, 4 and 5 on top of each other and then sew this set of six blocks to the left-hand side of the central rectangle.

Row 3 (right side): jkl; block + nine patch.

Row 4 (right side): nine patch + 'pqr' block.

Row 5 (right side): heart block + nine patch.

Sew the right-hand side rows 3, 4 and 5 on top of each other and sew this set of six blocks to the right-hand side of the central rectangle.

Row 6: nine patch + heart block + nine patch + 'stu' block + nine patch + heart block.

Row 7: 'vwx' block + nine patch + heart block + nine patch + 'yz' block + nine patch.

Now press the seams of the sewn rows open and carefully join them together as in Fig 2. Press the quilt and check its width – it should measure 36½in (92.7cm) wide.

Adding the border

See page 99 for adding borders. Cut two of your 2½in (6.3cm) strips to the quilt width and sew them to the top and bottom of the quilt. Make sure you pin the border to each end of the quilt first and then ease the rest in using lots of pins vertical with the seam. Press this seam open. The side of your quilt should now measure 50½in (128.3cm). Cut your two remaining strips to this measurement and join on to the quilt, as before. Sew and then press the seams open. Note: you may need to join the borders if your fabric was not wide enough.

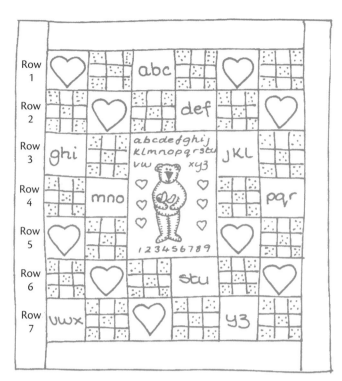

Fig 2 *Assembling the quilt blocks*

Sew the ⅝in (1.6cm) wide ribbon or tape to the outside edge of the centre panel. Start in one corner and mitre the corners as you go (see Fig 3). Sew the tape in position close to both edges. Using the same technique, sew the ½in (1.3cm) wide ribbon or tape (or the wider one if you prefer) around the quilt where the border joins the quilt.

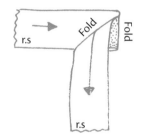

Fig 3 *Mitring the corners of the ribbon tape*

Layering the quilt

Cut a piece of fleece or minkie 45in x 52in (114.3cm x 132cm) for a backing and refer to page 100 for layering the quilt.

Quilting

Quilt, with a machine or by hand, around the inside of all the blocks and the central rectangle to stabilize the quilt. Quilt diagonally across all the nine-patch blocks (see picture detail, below left). Embroider the hearts, alphabets and numbers using backstitch (see page 102). The fleece on the back may hide your stitches so make sure you sew through to the back to quilt it.

Trim the borders to neaten. From the front edge tack (baste) and then sew on the ribbon tape. Sew close to the edge of the ribbon on the left side only, mitring the corners. The tape should be slightly proud of the quilt. Sew another round of tape to the wrong side. This will actually be sewn on to the wrong side of the front tape. Sew on the right-hand side of the tape only. Mitre the corners. Finish by slipstitching the tape in place on the wrong side of the quilt.

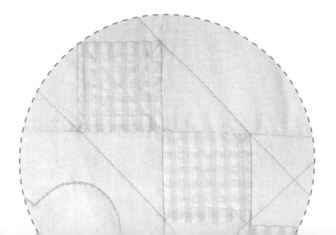

Ted Bear

This cute bear takes on a different character with every fabric you use. I like his mouse-like ears and strange little body, and once I'd made him I couldn't alter his defects because he was looking at me so lovingly. You could embellish a smooth fabric with hearts and letters. The finished size is 14in (35.5cm) tall.

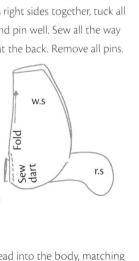

Ingredients

- o One fat quarter of fabric for bear
- o One bag of polyester stuffing
- o Two small black buttons ⁵⁄₁₆in (8mm) diameter
- o Skein of embroidery thread (optional)
- o Felt for nose 1in (2.5cm) square

1 Enlarge the templates on page 107 by 200% and cut out the patterns. Fold the fat quarter in half, right sides together. Pin the pattern pieces on the fabric and cut them out (you only need one gusset and two sets of ears). Make a note of special markings and openings. Set the machine up with matching thread top and bottom and reduce your stitch length. If embroidering hearts and letters (from the main quilt), transfer these marks now and backstitch with two strands of thread.

2 *Legs and arms:* place a pair of legs right sides together and sew, leaving a gap at the top and the back where indicated on the pattern. Repeat with the other leg and the two arms.

Head and ears: sew the ears together, turn right way out and top stitch around the ear curve. Fold the head in half along the ear dart, place the ear between the darts and pin. Sew, starting a ¼in (6mm) in from the edge (see Fig 1). Unfold the head, fold the ear forward on to the head and pin in position – this may appear odd but all will be revealed. Repeat with the other side of the head. Place the head pieces right sides together and sew from the nose down to the neck. Open out the seam. Find the centre of the nose on the gusset and pin this to the centre of the seam you have just sewn. With right sides together, pin one side of the neck end of the gusset to one side of the back of the head. Ease and pin the gusset to the side of the head and sew. Do each side separately.

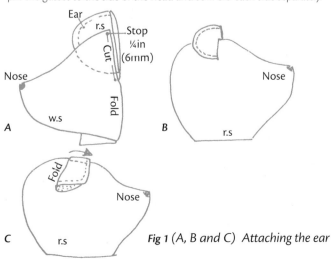

Fig 1 (A, B and C) Attaching the ear

3 *Body:* take one leg and place it into the leg dart, right sides together, with the toe of the leg facing down (Fig 2). Fold the body in half along this leg dart and sew the leg dart twice, incorporating a leg. Repeat with the other side. Tack the two arms in place along the neck edge as on the pattern. Place the two bodies right sides together, tuck all arms and legs into the middle of the body and pin well. Sew all the way around leaving an opening at the neck and at the back. Remove all pins.

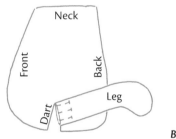

Fig 2 Attaching the leg (A and B)

4 Turn the head right way out. Pop the head into the body, matching front and back seams. Check all is well and sew by hand (it's a bit tricky by machine). Turn the bear the right way out via the back opening. Stuff the head first, quite firmly, followed by the body. Close the back opening with ladder stitch (see page 103). Loosely stuff the arms and legs. Ladder stitch the openings.

5 Cut out the nose in felt, pin in place and blanket stitch it on. Backstitch the mouth and philtrum (the bit between upper lip and nose). Use two buttons for eyes but sew them on *very* securely if you are giving the bear to a child, or embroider the eyes in satin stitch. Tie a little frayed scarf around the bear's neck and give with love!

Kitchen Cosies

My kitchen gets all the wear and tear in our home because we spend so much time in there, and sometimes it could do with a little love and care with a material girl's re-vamp. This chapter features a wonderful collection of kitchen necessities, all on a cute cupcake theme, and the bold red and white colour scheme, chunky stitching and jumbo ric-rac braid are sure to brighten up the dullest kitchen.

The kitchen accessories feature various techniques, which are all easy to do – a little appliqué, some crazy patchwork and the clever use of decorative braid and big, bold buttons. So make these most useful items, be the envy of your neighbourhood and reduce that fabric stash – all at the same time!

Re-vamping a kitchen couldn't be easier with this colourful collection of tea cosy, oven glove and tea towel. Who'd have thought cupcakes could be so versatile? See pages 32–34 for a darling little peg bag, seat cover and doorstop.

Oven Glove

I can't be without lots of these – one to use and one in the wash. You can now buy heat-resistant wadding, which is perfect for this project. The glove is made with an unusual but practical layering technique.

Finished size: 11½in x 7½in (29.2cm x 19cm)
Techniques: Using templates (page 96) • Fusible webbing (page 96) • Freezer paper (page 96) • Appliqué (page 98) • Ric-rac (page 99) • Binding (page 101)

Ingredients

o One fat quarter each of main fabric and lining
o One fat quarter of heat-resistant wadding (batting)
o Wide ric-rac braid 45in (114cm)
o Binding 22in x 1½in (56cm x 3.8cm)
o Co-ordinating fabric scraps for the appliqué cupcake
o Button for the cupcake 'cherry'

Quick Tip...
The layering up of this glove is unusual but I have constructed it this way so that the thick bulk of the layers won't slip and will be easier to sew.

1 Enlarge the oven glove template on page 108 by 200%. Trace the shape on to freezer paper, or make a cardboard template, and cut out. Fold the fat quarter for the lining in half right sides together. Cut two rectangles of wadding the same size as the folded fabric and place a rectangle on each side of the lining.

2 Enlarge the medium cupcake template on page 108 by 200%. Appliqué a cupcake into the middle of the folded half of the main fabric by tracing the cupcake pieces on to the smooth side of the fusible webbing. Cut the pieces out roughly, not on the traced line. Iron the fusible shapes on to the wrong side of your chosen fabrics (the smooth side of the paper will face the bottom of the iron). Cut the shapes out accurately on the line. Peel off the paper backing, put the shapes in place and iron them to fuse them to the fabric. Work blanket stitch (see page 102) around all of the appliqué pieces. (For more detailed instructions on appliqué see page 98.)

3 Fold the main fabric right sides together and either iron on the freezer paper template or use the cut-out template to mark the shape of the glove on to the fabric, using a pencil. When doing this make sure the cupcake is positioned centrally as it will be on the reverse at this moment.

4 Place the main, marked, folded fat quarter on top of the prepared lining and wadding (see Fig 1). Pin with large pins: this may not be what you were expecting but *do not cut*. Stitch on the marked line, leaving the bottom open.

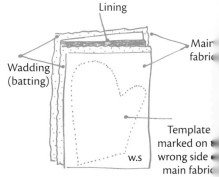

Fig 1 *Layering the glove*

5 Trim seams to a scant ¼in (6mm), snipping into the V of the thumb. Turn right way out via the main fabric. Check all seams are caught and that the thumb isn't snagged. Tack (baste) the ric-rac on to the bottom edge of the glove, making sure the ric-rac humps line up with the raw edge.

6 Bind the bottom edge, incorporating a folded tag for hanging up. With two strands of embroidery thread and a chunky stitch, quilt around the outside edge of the cupcake. Now get baking so you can try out the glove.

Tea Cosy

I recycle my tea bags and yet, after two years, the bags are still not composted although the tea has gone. So I say give up tea bags and go back to teapots, tea leaves and tea cosies – not plain, knitted ones but cupcake cosies!

Finished size: 8½in x 10in (21.6cm x 25.4cm)
Techniques: Using templates (page 96) • Fusible webbing (page 96) • Appliqué (page 98) • Ric-rac (page 99) • Binding (page 101)

Ingredients

o One fat quarter of lining fabric
o One fat quarter of heat-resistant wadding (batting) or ordinary wadding
o One fat quarter of fabric for cupcake (mine's brown)
o One fat quarter of fabric for cupcake case (mine's red)
o Scrap of cream fabric for icing
o Fusible webbing, such as Bondaweb
o Wide ric-rac braid 22in (56cm) long
o Packet of seed beads for 'hundreds and thousands'
o Binding fabric 20in x 2in (51cm x 5cm)
o Two large buttons 1½in (3.8cm) wide

1 Cut two 5in x 9in (12.7cm x 22.9cm) red rectangles for the base of the cupcake. To the right side top edges of each rectangle sew on a length of co-ordinating ric-rac braid (see page 99).

2 Enlarge the tea cosy templates (cake and icing) on page 108 by 200% on a photocopier. Using the brown fabric and cake template, cut two. For each side of the cosy, sew these to the rectangles. Press and stitch along the line of the ric-rac to hold it in place. Using the cream fabric and the icing template, cut two. Appliqué the icing fabric to the top of the cake using fusible webbing and blanket stitch (see page 102).

3 Cut two 10in x 12in (25.4cm x 30.5cm) rectangles of wadding and two of lining fabric. Place the lining pieces right sides together and put a piece of wadding on each side (see Fig 1). Put the two pieced cupcakes right sides together, place on to the wadding and pin well. Sew the cupcakes together through all layers using a ¼in (6mm) seam, leaving the bottom unsewn. Trim to a scant ¼in (6mm) and turn right way out via the cupcake. Check all seams have been sewn in and then bind all around the bottom opening.

4 Sew on beads for 'hundreds and thousands' (or embroider stitches if you prefer). Sew the two large buttons for a cherry through the top inch of the icing. Time to put the kettle on and make yourself a cup of tea – don't forget to put the cosy on the teapot!

12in (30.5cm)

10in (25.4cm)

Cupcake

w.s

Two lining pieces right sides together

Wadding

Fig 1
Assembling the tea cosy layers

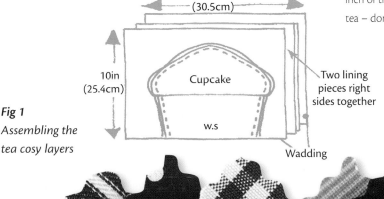

Peg Bag

This is the real McCoy, nostalgia at its finest, a peg bag from the 1950s – I'll have you wearing hair nets next!

Finished size: 15in x 13in (38cm x 33cm)
Techniques: Using templates (page 96) ● Fusible webbing (page 96) ● Appliqué (page 98) ● Ric-rac (page 99)

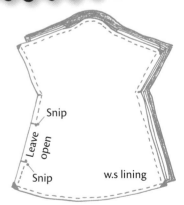

Ingredients

o Two different fabrics, two fat quarters of each
o Scraps of co-ordinating fabric for appliquéing a medium cupcake
o Wide ric-rac braid 45in (114cm) long
o Child's wooden coat hanger 13in (33cm) (or cut down an adult hanger)
o Large button for the 'cherry'

1 Enlarge the templates for the peg bag on page 109 by 200% on a photocopier. Cut out the patterns. Fold a main fabric and a lining fat quarter in half, wrong sides together, and place one on top of the other. Put the front pattern on top of the fabric, matching the pattern fold with the fabric fold. Pin well and cut out. Repeat for the back pattern.

2 Enlarge the medium cupcake template on page 108 by 200%. Appliqué the cupcake in place (see step 2 on page 30).

3 Using the guideline on the pattern, tack the ric-rac on to the right side of one of the front pieces, around the curved neck edge. Now tack the ric-rac to the bottom edge and to the two sleeve edges, where indicated on the pattern. Leave ½in (1.25cm) at each end of the ric-rac un-sewn and turn the ends back on themselves (not under) as this makes turning the right way out neater.

4 Place the two front pieces right sides together and sew, using the tacked line for the ric-rac as a guide. Trim to a scant ¼in (6mm). Turn the front pieces the right way out and press. Top stitch around the curved edge, sewing one line close to the edge and the next ¼in (6mm) away.

5 Place the two back pieces right sides together and put the front section between them, like a sandwich. Pin well, making sure all edges are matching. Sew all the way around, leaving an opening where indicated on the pattern. The seam allowance depends on the ric-rac width.

Snip

Leave open

Snip

w.s lining

Fig 1 *Layering the peg bag*

6 Snip up to the stitch line at each end of the opening. Do *not* trim this part of the seam but for all the other seams trim to a scant ¼in (6mm). Carefully snip under the 'armpits'. Turn the bag the right way out via the opening. You might have turned it with the wrong side of the ric-rac showing so put your hand into the bag and pull it out the right way. Pick out all corners and make sure all seams are caught in with the stitches.

7 Turn the bag the wrong way out and sew up the opening, trim slightly and then zigzag stitch to secure the raw edges. Turn the bag back the right way. Pop in your coat hanger, fill the bag with pegs, hang it on the line and sit back and admire!

Seat Cover

Kitchen chairs take a lot of abuse in our house: they double as ladders, playtime camps and even saw benches. I haven't trained my family very well because I'm too busy sewing! Put handmade cushion pads on your chairs and *perhaps* they will be treated with more respect.

Finished size: 13½in (34.3cm) diameter
Techniques: Fusible webbing (page 96) • Crazy stitch and flip (page 98) • Appliqué (page 98) • Ric-rac (page 99) • Decorative stitches (page 102)

Ingredients

- -

o One fat quarter of lining fabric
o One fat quarter of calico
o One fat quarter of thick wadding (batting)
o Ten scraps of co-ordinating fabrics (to include cupcake appliqué)
o Scraps of ric-rac braid and ribbon
o Webbing tape ½yd (0.5m) x ½in (1.25cm) wide, to tie seat cover to chair
o Wide ric-rac braid 46in (117cm) for edging
o Large button for the cupcake 'cherry'

1 First make a template of the chair you want a cushion pad on (see page 96 for advice), remembering to add on ¼in (6mm) for seam allowances. From your pattern cut out a piece of calico for the base of your crazy patchwork. Gather all the scraps and fabrics you want to use on the cushion and press them.

2 Cut a 5in (12.7cm) square out of the lightest fabric and appliqué on a small cupcake in the middle (see step 2 on page 30). Cut off all four corners roughly – it's best if they are all at slightly different angles. Pin this multi-sided patch in the middle of the calico right side up (making sure the cupcake is the right way up).

3 Lay one of the assorted strips or 'chunks' along one edge of the patch, right sides together and raw edges matching. Sew in place, trim off the extra length of the second fabric and flip it so it is right side up (see diagram on page 98) and press. Place a different strip on an adjacent edge of the multi-sided patch, pin and sew in place. Trim the excess, flip the new fabric to the right side and press. Continue in this way all the way around the multi-sided patch to cover the middle section of the calico, varying the angles. If there are any gaps that a strip won't cover, cut a square, turn under ¼in (6mm) on three sides (leaving the side hanging off the calico unhemmed) and pin in place. Top sew in place. When the calico is covered, press and then trim the edges of the patchwork even with the calico.

4 With wrong side down, lay the crazy patchwork on to a thick piece of wadding and either spray adhere this together (see page 95) or pin. Machine sew along the seams to quilt the patches. Decorate the seams between the crazy patchwork by sewing on braids, ric-racs and ribbons, using embroidery stitches like blanket stitch, chain stitch, herringbone stitch, running stitch and whip stitch. Sew on some wide ric-rac all the way around the outside edge.

5 Cut backing fabric 1in (2.5cm) larger than the cushion, place it right sides together with the patchwork and sew all the way around leaving a 4in (10.2cm) opening at the top. Trim all the seams to a scant ¼in (6mm) and turn the right way out, checking all seams have been caught. Slipstitch the opening closed.

6 Place the cushion on its chair and mark the positions of the ties with a pin. Cut two ties from ribbon or webbing tape and sew to the cushion. Voila, all done – just another five to make!

Doorstop

This doorstop is trendy, useful, fun and quick – half an hour from beginning to end.

Finished size: 7½in long x 5½in wide x 3½in deep (19cm x 14cm x 9cm)
Techniques: Appliqué (page 98) ● Ric-rac (page 99)

1 From the fat quarter cut a piece 18in x 12in (46cm x 30.5cm). Enlarge the medium cupcake templates on page 108 by 200%. Appliqué a cupcake to the right side of the fabric in the middle (see step 2 on page 30). With right sides together sew the longer seam with a smaller-than-normal stitch. Open out, so that the seam is in the middle of the rectangle and press to keep this seam in the middle. Sew along the bottom edge with a ¼in (6mm) seam. Reinforce this seam by sewing twice. Sew along the top edge leaving a 2½in (6.3cm) gap in the middle.

2 In all four corners cut out a 2in (5cm) square (see Fig 1). This measurement does *not* include the seam allowance you have just sewn. Starting with one corner of the bottom edge (the one without the gap), squash the bottom seam on to the side seam. Sew this seam twice. Repeat with the other side.

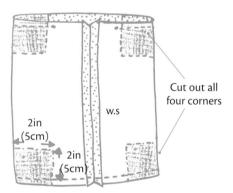

2in (5cm)

2in (5cm)

W.S

Cut out all four corners

Fig 1 *Cutting out the corners*

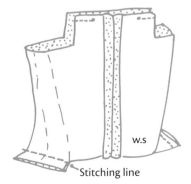

W.S

Stitching line

Fig 2 *Sewing across the bottom edge (sugar bagging)*

Ingredients

- o One fat quarter
- o Scraps of fabric for cupcake appliqué
- o Scraps of fusible webbing
- o Filling for doorstop, approx 2lbs (1kg) weight (e.g. plastic pellets, bird grit, dry-baked lentils or rice)
- o Small amount of polyester stuffing
- o Webbing tape for handle 6in x 2in (15.2cm x 5cm)
- o Wide ric-rac braid, about 6in (15.2cm) long
- o One large red button for 'cherry'

3 Take the 6in (15.2cm) strip of webbing tape and sew the ric-rac in place along the centre. Now sew the top of the doorstop in the same way as you did for the bottom, except that one end of the webbing tape handle is placed centrally into the squashed corner before sewing the seam twice. Repeat with the other side.

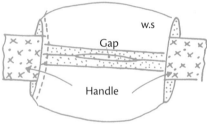

W.S

Gap

Handle

Fig 3 *Inserting the handle ends and sewing in place (overhead view)*

4 Turn the doorstop the right way out through the opening. Fill it nearly to the top with your filling and then finish off with some stuffing. Ladder stitch the opening closed (see page 103). All that remains is to find a door that needs propping open – or use it as a book end.

I am sure you've got the idea by now – go cupcake mad and decorate everything to your heart's content. Treat yourself to a set of new tea towels and decorate them with appliquéd cupcakes and bands of bright ric-rac braid.

Picnic Season

I have designed this rug and wine cooler to remind you just how pleasurable a simple picnic can be. There's nothing to compare with the delight of preparing some lovely grub, filling a flask with hot tea or coffee, packing your picnic rug, throwing in a ball and a bit of sewing. Pick up a granny on the way and pop down the road to the nearest beach or park. Let the kids go wild, read a book, sew or just sit and listen – lovely.

After our daughter's graduation, while everyone else dashed into the city to celebrate in some over-priced restaurant, we found the local park, laid out our rug and picnicked to our hearts' content… bliss. The rug is made from hard-wearing denim and is simplicity itself to make – just sixteen squares sewn together and edged with a wide border. Some appliquéd cupcakes provide a bright contrast. The wine cooler is also made from denim, with a cluster of decorative buttons. So all you need is a break in the weather and off you go!

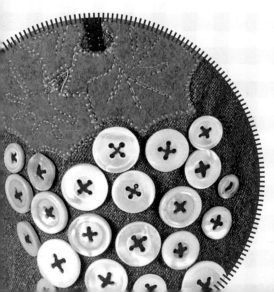

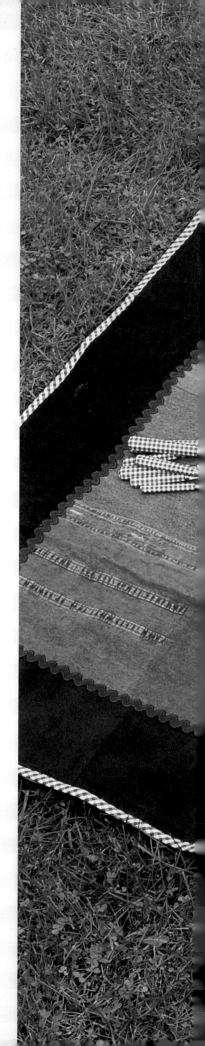

This rug is a great winner for picnics. It has four cute denim pockets, taken from children's clothes, to hold stone weights that anchor the rug when it's in use, and a larger denim pocket to hold napkins. It's easy to adapt to a quilt by putting wadding on the back and would be popular with young children and teenagers. A handy wine cooler ensures that wine stays crisp and cold.

Rugged Picnic Rug

This rug is so quick and easy to make. You'll discover how wonderful denim is to work with and might even be tempted to turn the rug into a full-blown quilt with a fleece back. The denim is best taken from shirts and skirts not heavy jeans, where it's unlikely you'll be able to cut many 10in (25.4cm) squares. Before you start cutting though, cut 6½in (16.5cm) strips from the bottom of the skirts or dresses for your borders. These can be joined and different colours and slight variations in weights are ideal.

Finished size: 52½in (133.3cm) square
Techniques: Using templates (page 96) ● Appliqué (page 98) ● Ric-rac (page 99) ● Borders (page 99)

Quick Tip. . .
If you can't get oilcloth, the fabric used for exterior tablecloths is fine, or use a ground sheet, often sold at army surplus stores.

Arranging the squares

1 Lay out the 10½in (26.7cm) squares of denim in four rows of four and then move them around until you have a nice balance of different coloured denims and make a note of this order.

Appliqué

2 Following the appliqué instructions in step 2 on page 30, and using the same templates (enlarged by 200% to full size), appliqué seven cupcakes, using fusible webbing, positioning them evenly over the squares of the rug.

3 Sew on the larger denim pocket in one of the denim squares, leaving the top open to house napkins (see picture below). If you prefer, place the pocket centrally, so people can reach it more easily.

Ingredients

- -

o Sixteen 10½in (26.7cm) squares of lightweight denim
o Strips of denim for borders:
  two pieces 6½in (16.5cm) wide x 40½in (102.9cm) long;
  two pieces 6½in (16.5cm) wide x 52½in (133.3cm) long
o Four small denim pockets from children's clothes
o One large denim pocket
o Scraps of fabric for cupcakes, in cream, light tan and red check
o Oilcloth 54in (137.2cm) square (see Quick Tip above)
o Nine large buttons for the rug, six for the rug handle and seven smaller ones for the 'cherries' on the cupcakes
o Binding 6yd (5.5m)
o Wide ric-rac braid 5yd (4.5m) long
o Scraps of Bondaweb
o Spray adhesive
o Velcro (hook and loop tape) for handle 8in (20.3cm)
o Webbing for handle 1in (2.5cm) wide x 53in (134.6cm) long

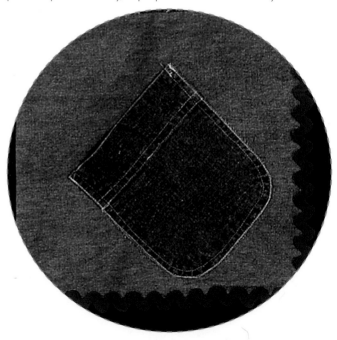

4 Sew your squares together in four rows of four, opening out seams as you go. Sew the four rows together, matching seams. Don't worry too much about the joins, as they will be hidden by a button.

The layout of the picnic rug – really just a large sixteen-patch block with some appliqué and ric-rac decoration, plus a wide border and some useful pockets.

Adding the border

5 Using ¼in (6mm) seams, sew two borders on to the top and bottom of the rug, each 6½in x 40½in (16.5cm x 102.9cm). Sew on the two remaining borders 6½in x 52½in (16.5cm x 133.3cm) to the sides of the rug. Press well and then sew on ric-rac on the seam line between the borders and the squares.

6 Place the small pockets into the four corners of the border, and sew in place, leaving the pocket tops open.

Backing

7 Cut your oilcloth or ground sheet 54in (137.2cm) square. Lay the quilt on top of the oilcloth, wrong sides together. It will be impossible to pin or tack these two layers together so use spray adhesive. Spray it lightly on to the oilcloth first and then press the two layers together. If using oilcloth, you will not be able to quilt the rug, so fix both layers together by sewing buttons to the nine middle joins.

Binding

8 Trim the quilt back to match the front. Cut your binding 2in (5cm) wide, iron it in half along its length and iron under a ¼in (6mm) one side and ½in (1.3cm) on the other. When the binding is sewn on, you will be attaching the binding and mitring the corners all in one go (see Fig 1).

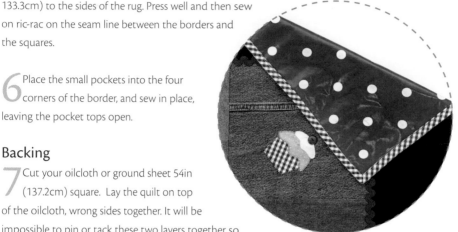

Quick tip
For a fast solution to the rug handle you could buy two small cat or dog collars and attach a lead between the two – there are some really lovely ones in pet stores.

Making the handle

9 Cut two lengths of webbing 21in (53.4cm) long and one 12in (30.5cm). Hem each end of the longer lengths. Sew one end of the smaller length of webbing to the middle of one of the longer lengths (see Fig 2). Repeat on the other side of the smaller length. Sew a 4in (10.2cm) piece of Velcro, a male and female, to each end of the longer lengths, one on the right side and one on the wrong side. Sew buttons along the smaller length to decorate. Fold and roll up your rug. Wrap the longer lengths around the rug, secure with the Velcro and swing by the handle!

Fold

Fold

½in
(1.3cm)

¼in
(6mm)

Binding

r.s

Fold

A

Velcro

Velcro

Fig 2 Making the carrying strap and handle

Folded
mitre

r.s

B

Binding

Fig 1 Attaching the binding (A) and mitring the corners as you go (B)

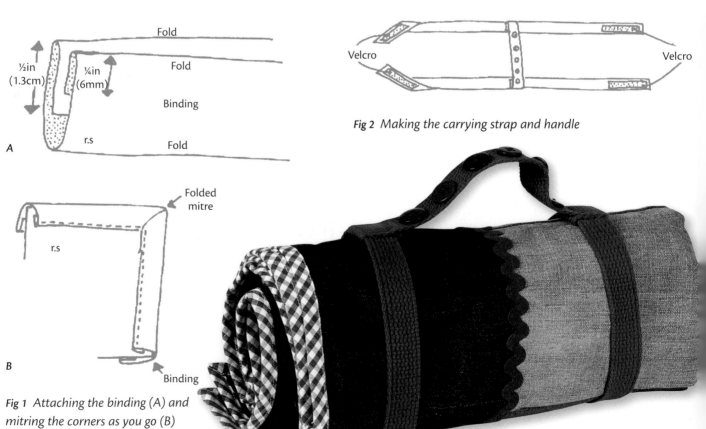

Grape Wine Cooler

Nothing is worse than warm white wine at a picnic; it must be icy cold and this wine cooler will solve the problem, especially if you use insulating wadding (batting). It is also a perfect gift wrap for a bottle of wine to give to friends. The finished size is 13in x 6in (33cm x 15.2cm).

Ingredients

o Main fabric 12½in x 14½in (31.7cm x 36.8cm)
o Insulating wadding (batting) 12½in x 14½in (31.7cm x 36.8cm)
o Lining fabric 12½in x 16½in (31.7cm x 41.9cm)
o Wide ric-rac braid 12½in (31.7cm)
o Green felt 10in (25.4cm) square
o Brown felt 2in (5cm) square
o Thirty assorted pearly buttons
o Tape or ribbon 18in (45.7cm) long

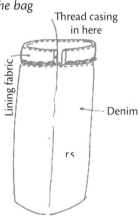

1 Cut a piece of denim and wadding each 12½in x 14½in (31.7cm x 36.8cm). Enlarge the leaf and stalk templates on page 109 by 200% and use the patterns to cut out three leaves from green felt and the stalk from brown felt. Appliqué the leaves and stalk in the middle of the denim fabric using blanket stitch (see page 102). Pin the piece of wadding to the wrong side of the denim. Sew a length of ric-rac to the top edge of the denim fabric.

2 Take the piece of lining fabric and measure 2in (5cm) down from the top at each end and ½in (1.3cm) in from the side and cut where shown on Fig 1. Fold this flap to the wrong side and top stitch.

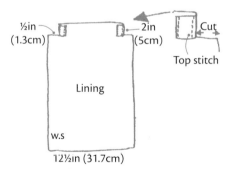

Fig 1 Cutting into the lining and folding the flaps over

3 Place the lining and outside fabric right sides together and sew along the top edge where the ric-rac and folded sides are. Open out and press. Top stitch along the ric-rac edge. Fold the fabric in half vertically, matching seams, and sew along the long edge leaving a 4in (10.2cm) gap in the lining seam (see Fig 2). Squash the bottle cooler so the seam is in the middle and sew along the top and bottom edge.

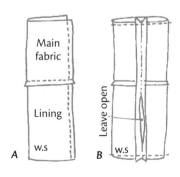

Fig 2 Creating the bottle shape

4 'Sugar bag' bottom all four corners by squashing the side seam on to the bottom seam. Measure in 2in (5cm) and sew across (see Fig 3).

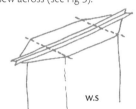

Fig 3 'Sugar bagging' the bottom of the bag

5 Turn the right way out via the opening in the lining seam. Push the lining into the main fabric. Press and pin the top edge so that the lining protrudes. Top stitch at the top and bottom of the protruding lining to make the casing (see Fig 4). Thread 18in (45.7cm) of tape or ribbon through the casing. To make the handle, cut a 12in (30.5cm) length of tape. Turn under a ½in (1.3cm) hem at both ends and attach to the back seam of the wine cooler with a button, sewing through all layers.

6 Sew on pearly buttons beneath the leaves and through to the lining to resemble a bunch of grapes. Add a few buttons to the back tape too. All done – don't forget the cork screw!

Fig 4 Creating the casing

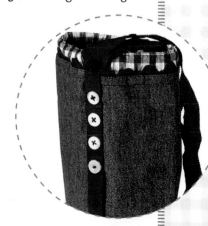

Quilt Show Shopper

Don't you just love going to quilt shows? I love nosing around the little local ones checking out the sampler quilts. I try to attend at least one large show each year and am always amazed at the quality of some of the work: how do they do that 600 stitches to the inch thing, and claim to work full time, have ten kids, a loving husband and be a micro surgeon or something – wow?!

One of my favourite shows is in February at a local agricultural showground. It's quirky and cosy; we've had the mad rush of Christmas, the weather is getting us down and we all need a boost of inspiration in the quilting department. In our quilt group it became a sort of tradition to make a bag to show off and fill up. You can share this tradition with me and make this bright and breezy bag to take to your next show. The sides are simply pieced strips, with a hard-wearing fabric for the base and lower sides. There's also a handy little matching purse, perfect for fabric swatches – see instructions on page 47.

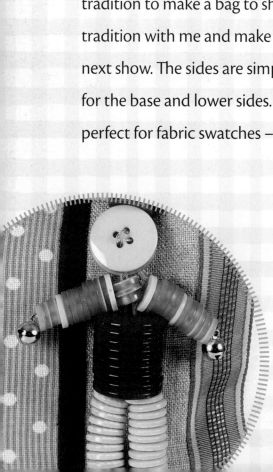

This colourful bag is roomy and so useful – all you need is a few bright fabric strips, some bits of trim and off you go on your shopping trip. The jingling dolly button charm is a sweet idea and very easy to make.

Strippy, Stripy Bag

This is a roomy bag for you to fill up at your local quilt show. I used a bright Kaffe Fassett floral to line mine because I like a nice surprise when I look in a bag. The bottom of the bag uses a hardwearing deck chair fabric. You'll be amazed at the amount of compliments you'll get and the great satisfaction from saying, 'Thank you, I made it'. Turn the radio on, make a cup of tea and away we go!

Finished size: 14in x 18½in (35.5cm x 47cm) approx
Techniques: Ric-rac (page 99)

Quick Tip. . .
You can use any trims you like, such as ribbons, braids and ric-racs, in varying widths – just make sure the colours tone with your bag fabrics.

Making the bag

1 The layout of the bag is shown in Fig 1. Begin by cutting up the five different fabrics into 2½in x 8½in (6.3cm x 21.6cm) strips. Mix and match them and then join them together, using ¼in (6mm) seams, in two sets of ten to make two sides. Decorate each seam by sewing on the ribbons and braids. Sew a piece of wide ric-rac or lace on the bottom end of each side.

Ingredients

For the bag
- o Fabric for bottom of bag and handles ¾yd (0.75m)
- o Five different fabrics for pieced stripes each 12in x 8½in (30.5cm x 21.6cm)
- o Lining fabric 1yd (1m)
- o Five different trims to decorate the pieced stripes, each 20in (50.8cm) long
- o Two magnetic poppers
- o D-ring or swivel clip (to hang keys on)
- o Stiff cardboard 7in x 12in (17.8cm x 30.5cm)
- o Fabric 14½in x 12½in (36.8cm x 31.8cm) to cover cardboard
- o Tape 4in x 1in (10.2cm x 2.5cm)

For the button dolly
- o Twenty-four buttons ⁵⁄₁₆in (8mm) diameter for arms
- o Twenty-four buttons ⅜in (10mm) diameter approx for legs
- o Nine buttons ¹³⁄₁₆in (20mm) diameter for body
- o Three buttons ¼in (6mm) diameter for neck
- o Two buttons 1in (25mm) diameter for head
- o One button ⅜in (10mm) diameter for hat
- o Two lengths of fine cord or thong each 25in (63.5cm) long
- o Four small bells

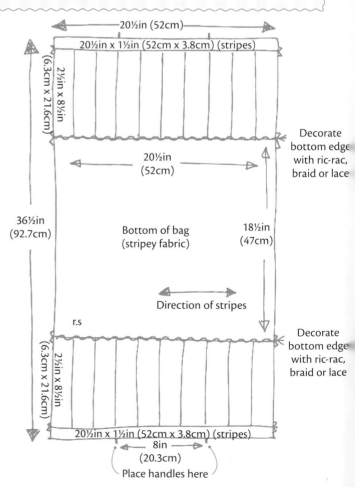

Fig 1 The layout of the bag before assembly

2 Cut out the bottom of the bag 20½in x 18½in (52cm x 47cm). Join the two sides to each end of the bottom of the bag. At each end of the top of the pieced stripes sew a narrow strip 20½in x 1½in (52cm x 3.8cm) (see Fig 1).

3 From the stripy fabric cut a rectangle 12in x 18in (30.5cm x 45.7cm) for the inner pocket. Fold in half with right sides together and sew all the way around leaving a gap in the bottom (see Fig 2A). Snip the corners, turn right way out and press. Decorate the top edge with ric-rac and then top stitch. Cut a piece of lining 20½in x 36½in (52cm x 92.7cm). Place the pocket on to the right side of the lining 3½in (8.9cm) from the top edge. Centralize the pocket and pin in place (Fig 2B). Attach a magnetic fastener to the pocket and the lining following the manufacturer's instructions. Top stitch the pocket in place.

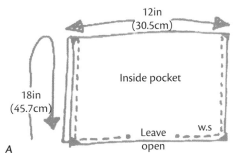

A

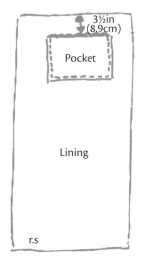

B

Fig 2 *Making the inner pocket (A) and positioning the pocket on the lining (B)*

4 Cut two handles from your stronger fabric 3¼in x 15in (8.3cm x 38.1cm). Using an iron, press ¼in (6mm) on one side and 1in (2.5cm) in on the other, fold in half and pin. Sew down the length of each side of the handle and then sew one line straight down the middle. Pin the handles on to the bag at each end as indicated on Fig 1, checking that they are not twisted. They are placed to the right side of the bag.

Using the piece of 4in (10.2cm) tape, thread on the D-ring and fold the tape in half. Pin the tape and D-ring to the right side of one of the top edges of the bag. When you continue with the construction of the bag, the tape will be automatically sewn in.

Quick Tip. . .

Bags can be made from any fabric: the stronger upholstery types are ideal but if you have fallen in love with a finer cotton mostly used for patchwork, stabilize the fabric with iron-on interfacing such as Vilene. Alternatively, use a thin cotton wadding (batting) between the lining and exterior fabric.

5 Place the lining right sides together with the bag. Sew the top and bottom seam only. Open out and re-fold, so that the bag is right sides with the other half of the bag, and the lining is sitting right sides to the other half of the lining (see Fig 3A). Match all the side seams carefully and pin well. At the bottom of the bag end, tuck up and fold under 4in (10.2cm). This will create an unusual square corner on the right side when you turn the bag right way out (Fig 3B). Pin well. Sew both side seams leaving a gap in one, at the lining end.

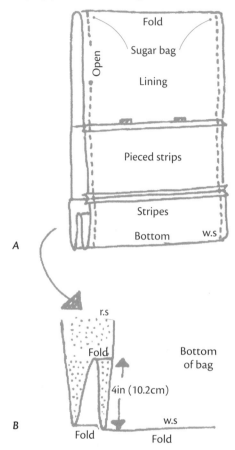

Fig 3 *Assembling the main bag (A) and folding the bag bottom (B)*

6 'Sugar bag bottom' the lining end only, by squashing the side seam on to the bottom seam (you do not actually have a seam here but an imaginary one, so you might find it useful to mark it with a pin). Sew a straight line 2½in (6.3cm) in from the end (see Fig 4). Do this at both ends of the lining. Turn the right way out via the opening and push the lining into the bag. While you still have access to the inside, attach your magnetic catch to the thin top edge, following the manufacturer's instructions. Sew closed the opening in the lining. Top stitch around the top edge of the bag on the thin, narrow strip.

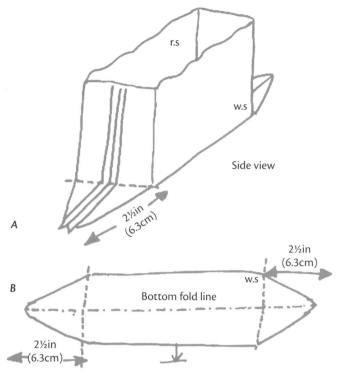

Fig 4 *'Sugar bagging' the lining: A shows the side view, while B shows the bottom view*

7 Take the piece of fabric for covering the cardboard and fold it in half. Sew a short and long side and turn the right way out. Place the cardboard inside the opening and slipstitch closed. Place this in the bottom of the bag for stability.

Making the button dolly

8 Take one length of fine cord or thong and fold it in half. Thread a bell into the middle of the fold. Using the two ends of the cord, thread through twelve 10mm buttons. Repeat with the other leg. Thread the two strands of one leg up into one hole of a 20mm button. Repeat with the other leg. Then thread both cords through the remaining eight 20mm buttons for the body.

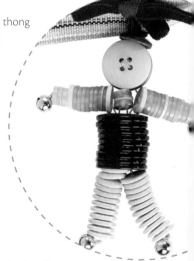

9 Taking one strand of the cord only, thread into one hole of the twelve 8mm buttons for an arm, into a bell and back up through the buttons. Repeat for the other arm. Thread both sets of cord into the two 6mm buttons for the neck. Take one set of arm and leg cords and thread them in and out of the two head buttons, placed wrong sides together, and do the same with the other sets of cord. Bring all cords out between the two head buttons at the top and thread through a hat button and fasten off securely. Thread a piece of ribbon under your fastening off to attach the dolly to the bag. There you are all done and dusted. Fill your bag and use with delight.

Swatch Purse

I can't have enough of these things: some girls have shoes, I have purses. I made this one especially for taking to quilt shops or shows, to keep swatches of fabric in that I am trying to match. The finished size is approximately 6in x 10in (15.2cm x 25.4cm).

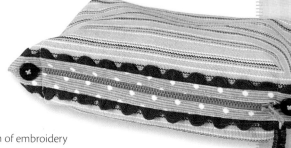

Ingredients

o One fat quarter of main fabric
o One fat quarter of lining fabric
o Zip (zipper) 10in (25.4cm) long
o Wide ric-rac 21in (53.3cm) long
o Twelve small buttons for zip pull

1 Cut four pieces of fabric 10½in x 6½in (26.7cm x 16.5cm), two in main and two in lining. Place a main piece and a lining piece wrong sides together and tack (baste) on a piece of ric-rac to the top edge (see Fig 1).

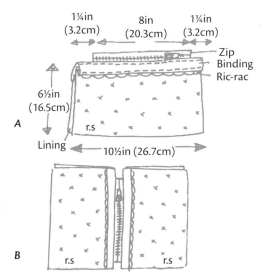

Fig 1 *Sewing the purse and lining pieces together (A). B shows the top view*

2 Cut two pieces of fabric 1¾in x 10½in (4.4cm x 26.7cm) to use as a binding. Bind the top edge of both sides where the ric-rac is. Place one side of the zip under one bound edge, centrally. Using a zipper foot, stitch close to the teeth. Place the other side of the purse on to the other side of the zip and sew in place as before.

3 Open out the lining, so right sides are together, and do the same with the main fabric sides – this will look a bit awkward but don't worry. Sew the main fabric together and the lining, leaving a gap to turn through (Fig 2A). You will not be able to sew over the zip so stop before it, as indicated in the diagram. 'Sugar bag bottom' all four corners, by squashing the side seam on to the bottom seam, and then sewing across the point (B). Sew 1½in (3.8cm) down from the point and then cut off the points.

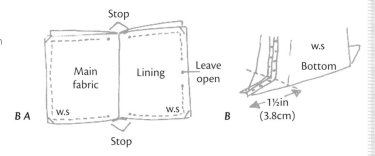

Fig 2 *Sewing the main fabric and lining together (A) and then 'sugar bagging' the lining (B)*

4 Turn right way out via the gap in the lining and stitch the opening closed. With extra strong thread, close the openings at either end of the zip with ladder stitch (see page 103). 'Sugar bag bottom' the ends on either side of the zip (this will not be quite as easy as before). Sew a button on each end of the points.

5 Thread a length of embroidery thread into the hole of the zip pull, thread on twelve small buttons and then tie off. Trendy, hey? Fill the purse with your swatches and notes to yourself and then find a quilt show to visit!

Celebration Time

I have always made a huge thing of birthdays and celebrations, putting gallons of time and energy into making and organizing really special events. We hire the local hall, send out handmade invitations, spend hours making sweet and sticky birthday cakes, researching wacky party games and decorating the home from top to bottom. From the moment that birthday girl or boy wakes up, they are Queen or King for the day.

Now that our girls are growing up and leaving home, I thought I could tone things down, but oh no, they expect it even more, saying it's all part of their childhood and memories. So I designed some little quilts and bunting for them to have in their new homes, when we can't all be together on special days. A girly version is shown opposite and described overleaf, and a boy's wall hanging and bunting, made in a similar way, is shown on page 53. The wall hangings are small and easy to make, and great fun to decorate with buttons, trims and embroidery stitches.

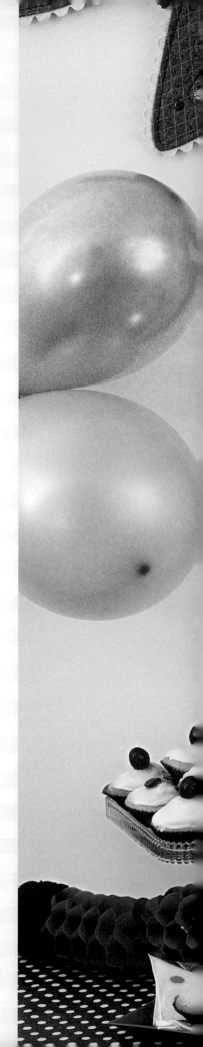

This sweet little wall hanging is easy to adapt for all sorts of celebrations – see a boy version on page 53 and baby and wedding wall hangings on pages 54 and 55.

Birthday Girl Wall Hanging

There are four lovely wall hangings in this chapter to celebrate special occasions – a birthday girl, birthday boy, a new baby and a wedding. The instructions detail the making of the birthday girl wall hanging and you can use these to create the other designs – or new ones of your own. The templates are provided for all four designs, beginning on page 110.

Finished size: 18½in x 22½in (47cm x 57.1cm)
Techniques: Using templates (page 96) ● Fusible webbing (page 96) ● Appliqué (page 98) ● Ric-rac (page 99) ● Adding borders (page 99) ● Binding (page 101)

Ingredients

- -

o Backing fabric 24in x 20in (61cm x 50.8cm)
o Border fabric ¼yd (0.25m) (a thin quarter)
o Fabric scraps for background (Strips A, B, C, D)
  2½in x 12½in (6.3cm x 31.8cm) for the name strip;
  8½in x 12½in (21.6cm x 31.8cm) to look like wallpaper;
  3½in x 12½in (8.9cm x 31.8cm) to look like a tablecloth;
  3½in x 12½in (8.9cm x 31.8cm) for cupcakes
o Scraps of co-ordinating fabrics for bunting, balloons, clothes and cakes
o Cotton wadding (batting) 20in x 24in (50.8cm x 61cm)
o Binding ¾in (1.9cm) wide x 2½yd (2.5m)
o Fusible webbing ¼yd (0.25m)
o Ric-rac braid ½in (1.3cm) wide x 1½yd (1.5m)
o Ric-rac braid ⅛in (3mm) wide x 1yd (1m) for bunting and balloons
o Seven small buttons for bunting
o Various flower and heart buttons and beads for decorations

1 Cut four strips for the background of the quilt, from the top (see the quilt layout picture opposite):
Strip A = 2½in x 12½in (6.3cm x 31.75cm).
Strip B = 8½in x 12½in (21.6cm x 31.75cm) – this fabric is for 'wallpaper'.
Strip C = 3½in x 12½in (8.9cm x 31.75cm) – this fabric is for a 'tablecloth'.
Strip D = 3½in x 12½in (8.9cm x 31.75cm).
Sew the four background strips together, in A, B, C, D order with ¼in (6mm) seams. Press seams open. Now cut the borders 3½in wide – two 12½in (31.75cm) long and two 22½in (57.1cm) long.

Appliqué

2 Using fusible webbing and the appliqué instructions on page 98, appliqué the name, bunting, girl (or boy) and the cakes in place. Use the templates on page 110, enlarging them by 200%. Use the girl photo opposite (and the boy photo on page 53) as a reference guide for the positions of each shape. Use the capital letter templates on page 110 to create the name of your choice. The letters already appear in reverse, so when you use them they will be the right way round.

3 Decorate the seams with ric-rac or ribbon between strips A and B, and C and D. Decorate the central panel with ric-rac, cutting two pieces 13in (33cm) long and two 17in (43.2cm) long. Place the ric-rac on all four sides making sure that when you tack through the middle of the ric-rac it is a ¼in (6mm) away from the raw edge. This may mean that the ric-rac overlaps the edge a little bit, but this is fine. When you come to sew on the borders with a ¼in (6mm) seam only half of the humps of the ric-rac will show and this is what we want (see Fig 1).

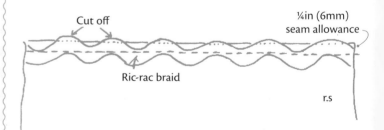

Cut off ¼in (6mm) seam allowance

Ric-rac braid

r.s

Fig 1 *Attaching the ric-rac braid around the centre panel*

The Birthday Girl Wall Hanging, with the different parts of the quilt identified. The other wall hangings in this chapter have the same basic layout.

Adding the border

4 Sew on the top and bottom borders, press, and then add the two side borders. Appliqué the balloons on to the borders using the templates on page 110 (enlarged by 200%). Add ric-rac 'strings'.

Layering

5 Cut backing fabric and cotton wadding (batting) each 24in x 20in (61cm x 50.8cm) and see page 100 for layering instructions.

Quilting and binding

6 Quilt, by machine or hand, around the inside of the borders and then along each strip. Now comes the fun bit as you decorate the crown, birthday cake, and bunting with buttons, beads, threads and ribbons. I used Pigma permanent pens for drawing the facial features, which are available in various colours and with fine and medium tips. I hand blanket stitched (see page 102) around the boy, girl, bunting and cupcakes. If your quilt needs a little extra you can add another line of ric-rac before you put on the binding. Tack (baste) it on in the same way as you did before. Bind the wall hanging using a double binding 2¾in (7cm) wide, and referring to the instructions on page 101.

Make this bold Birthday Boy Wall Hanging in the same way as the girl wall hanging but using appropriately piratical fabrics and the templates on page 110. Create the boy's name using the letter templates on page 110 and embellish with pirate-themed charms. To make the bunting follow the instructions on page 56, using the templates on page 111.

There are many wonderful fabrics featuring themed prints. As you can see here, I used a birthday cake print for the back of the girl's wall hanging and a Treasure Island theme for the boy's.

Make this pretty little wall hanging for a new baby in the same way
as the birthday wall hangings but using pastel fabrics of your choice and
the templates on page 111. Create the baby's name using the letter
templates on page 110 and 111 and add the date in backstitch using the
numbers on page 110.

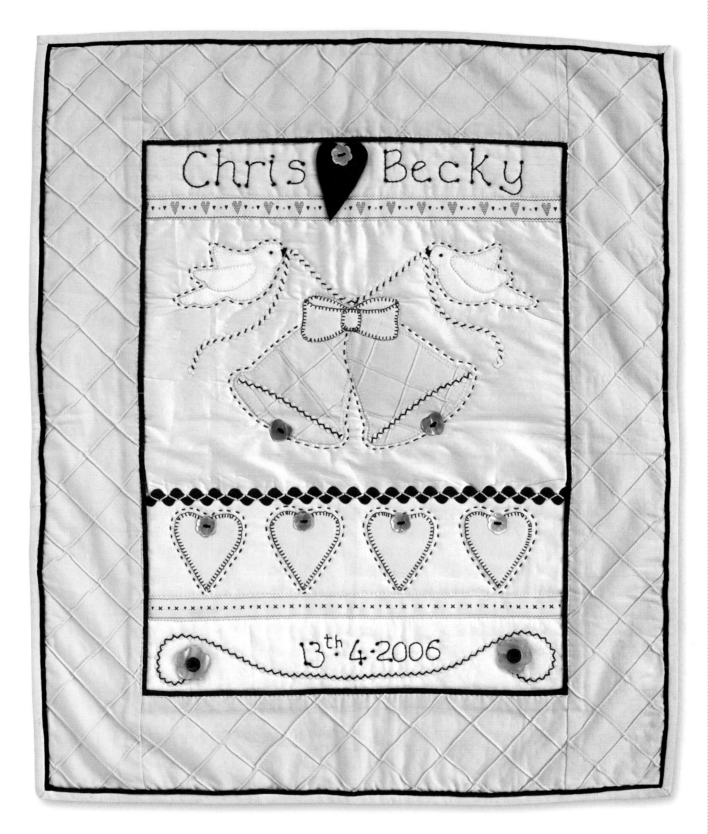

This elegant wall hanging is perfect as a wedding gift. It is made in a similar way to the other wall hangings but using cream fabrics, red embellishments and the templates on page 111. Create the names and date in backstitch, using the letter and numbers templates on page 110.

Celebration Bunting

Making your own bunting is great fun and useful for all sorts of occasions, adding a real hand-crafted look to your home. Instead of having names on the bunting, you could have a saying like 'Happy Birthday' or 'Congratulations'. The Birthday Girl bunting is described below but the instructions can also be used for the boy bunting shown on page 53, and using the templates on page 111.

Finished size: The flags are 7in (17.8cm) deep; the bunting length depends on the number of flags used
Techniques: Using templates (page 96) ● Fusible webbing (page 96) ● Freezer paper (page 96) ● Appliqué (page 98) ● Ric-rac (page 99) ● Binding (page 101)

Ingredients

o   Main fabric (one fat quarter makes eight flags)
o   Lining fabric fat quarter
o   Thin cotton wadding (batting)
o   Scraps of fabric for the cupcakes
o   Wide ric-rac braid, each flag needs 18in (45.7cm)
o   Binding
o   Buttons to decorate cupcakes and flags
o   Fusible webbing
o   Co-ordinating embroidery thread

Making the bunting

1 Enlarge the templates on page 111 by 200% and cut out the number of flags for the name you are using for the bunting, plus two for the balloons at each end. Use either a single fabric or all different ones. Cut flags from the lining fabric and also from the thin cotton wadding, but make sure they are ½in (1.3cm) bigger all the way around to allow for any discrepancies later on.

2 Using fusible webbing and the appliqué instructions on page 98, appliqué the letters of your chosen name, plus two balloons, on to the main fabric of the flags. The alphabets on pages 110 and 111 already have the letters reversed for you. Blanket stitch (see page 102) each letter by hand or machine.

3 Cut the wide ric-rac into 18in (44.7cm) long pieces for each flag and sew the ric-rac to the right side of the main flags. Make sure the edge of the ric-rac lines up with the edge of the bunting. *Do not sew along the top edge* (see page 99 for using ric-rac). When you come to sew around the bottom of the bunting, gently ease around the curve. With the wrong side of the flag facing you (the one with the ric-rac attached), place it on top of the lining, right sides together and place both of these on top of the cotton wadding (batting). Centralize the bunting into the

middle of the wadding. Pin well and sew, using the line of stitching you used to sew the ric-rac on as a guide. Sew all the way around but not along the top edge. Trim your seams to a scant ¼in (6mm) – this may mean cutting off some of the ric-rac.

4 Turn the flags the right way out and press well. Top stitch ¼in (6mm) in from the edge of the bunting either by hand or machine. Quilt around each letter with a co-ordinating thread. Attach a piece of ric-rac for the 'string' of the balloons.

5 Cut a length of binding 3in (7.6cm) wide x the length of your bunting + 12in (30.5cm) for tying it up at each end. Cut a piece of ric-rac the same length as your binding. Leave the first 6in (15.2cm) free and then sew the ric-rac to the top of the flags. You should have about 6in (15.2cm) overhang on each end. Lay the binding right side to the flags and sew it on with a ¼in (6mm) seam, or one that is appropriate to the ric-rac. Sew the binding on to the ric-rac at the beginning and at the end. Press, turn over and slipstitch in place. Turn under the ends of the ric-rac for a neat finish.

Adding the decorations

6 I've used cupcakes for the girl's bunting and skull and crossbones for the boy's. When the decorations are finished, attach them to the binding with a stitch of your choice or fabric glue.

Cupcakes: enlarge the templates on page 111 by 200% on a photocopier and cut out or trace the main cupcake template on to freezer paper. Mark or iron the template on to the wrong side of a piece of 'cup' fabric. Mark as many as you need on to the fabric with ½in (1.3cm) between each shape. Place another piece of the same fabric underneath the marked one, right sides together and sit these two on top of a piece of thin cotton wadding. *Do not cut.* Pin the three layers together with a few pins. Stitch all the way around the outside of each shape and then trim to a neat scant ¼in (6mm).

Cut a slit in the middle of one of the sides, as indicated on the pattern, and turn the right way out. There is no need to sew the opening closed as you will appliqué the 'cake' on to it in a moment. Using fusible webbing, appliqué the cake and then the icing on to the cup. Blanket stitch by hand or machine. Decorate with a button for the 'cherry' on the cake.

Skull and crossbones: these are made in the same way as the cupcakes using the templates on page 111 enlarged by 200%. I hand blanket stitched around the outside of each balloon and on the crossbones as they were a little fiddly for the machine. Hand sew on a 6in (15.2cm) piece of ribbon or ric-rac around the neck of the balloon for its string. I got a little carried away and sewed on lots of buttons across the top to decorate the binding and give the colour a lift. It's not totally necessary but it does look good!

Quick Tip...
You can decorate your bunting with any shape you like. The Christmas bunting on page 92 uses stars, snowmen, gingerbread men and holly.

Dancing Angels

This quilt was inspired by the golden angels on sale in the annual Nuremberg Christmas markets, a long-standing tradition in Germany. This is a delightful and impressive quilt to make, suitable for the keen beginner and the experienced stitcher alike – and also those who are passionate about angels. The central panel requires a touch of fiddly cutting and a fine blanket stitch, either by hand or machine, but once you have done that the five borders fly on and it's finished in no time. You'll also have a lot of fun adding decorative elements such as buttons and braids, plus some hand and machine quilting.

A gorgeous angel doll called Anja and her little dog Ron have also been made in a similar colour scheme – something to be treasured by all little girls (and big ones too!). See page 65 for the instructions for Anja and Ron.

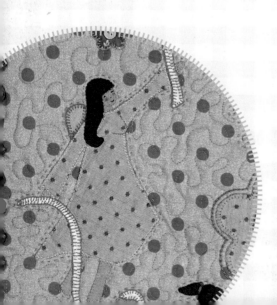

This beautifully coloured quilt is quite simple to make and the little angels in the centre panel are great fun to dress. There's also the sweetest angel doll to accompany the quilt (see page 65).

Dancing Angels Quilt

The inspiration for a quilt can come from anywhere. This lovely quilt was inspired by a German folk tale I found in an old book. About 300 years ago a doll maker made an angel doll for his grief-stricken wife who had lost their first child the night before Christmas. While absent-mindedly whittling at a piece of wood he noticed it resembled his lost child. He painted it gold and left it by his wife's bedside and when she woke she was greatly comforted. He continued to make these little carvings and they are now a tradition at the Nuremberg Christkindlesmarkt.

Finished size: 52in x 52in (132cm x 132cm)
Techniques: Using templates (page 96) ● Tea dyeing (page 96) ● Fusible webbing (page 96) ● Appliqué (page 98) ● Folded Flying Geese (page 10) ● Ric-rac (page 99) ● Adding borders (page 99) ● Binding (page 101)

Ingredients

- o   One fat quarter of fabric for Border 1 (a strong colour)
- o   One fat quarter of textured fabric
- o   Five fat eighths of main colour fabric (mine were pinks)
- o   Five fat eighths of secondary colour (mine were greens)
- o   Showcase fabric (pink dots) ¾yd (0.75m)
- o   Border fabric (pink pin-tucks) 1yd (1m)
- o   Scraps of tea-dyed calico for faces
- o   Scraps of brown fabric for hair
- o   Ric-rac braids (all optional):
  2yd (2m) x ⅜in (1cm) wide, (dark green) for central panel;
  6yd (5.5m) x ⅜in (1cm) wide, (light green) for Border 3;
  7yd (6.5m) x ⅜in (1cm) wide, (dark green) for outer edge
- o   Fusible webbing ½yd (0.5m)
- o   Assorted buttons and beads for decoration
- o   Three skeins of embroidery thread to match for quilting and embroidery and sewing on buttons
- o   100 pearl buttons and 50 small buttons to match
- o   Backing fabric 1½yd (1.5m) square
- o   Cotton/mix wadding (batting) 1½yd (1.5m) square
- o   Binding fabric 6½yd (6m)

1 Prepare your fabrics and read through the relevant technique sections from pages 96–101. The folded Flying Geese are made in the same way as in the Welcome Quilt – see page 10.

Stitching the centre panel

2 Cut out a 17½in (44.5cm) square from the fabric you are using for the quilt centre. This is bigger than needed to allow for shrinkage during appliqué and will be cut to size later. Enlarge the templates on pages 112–113 by 200%. Trace the patterns, angels and flowers for the central panel on to the smooth side of the fusible webbing, leaving ½in (1.25cm) between all pieces. Cut these out roughly and iron them on to the wrong side of your fabrics. Now cut the pieces out neatly on the line.

> *Quick Tip...*
> Once I have traced all the parts of one angel I draw a circle around it so that I don't get any clothing mixed up.

Binding

Border 5

Border 4

Border 3

Border 2

Border 1

Central Panel

1

2

5

3

4

*This beautifully coloured quilt is simpler than it looks. One of the
secrets is to choose a pre pleated fabric for the outer border.*

3 Arrange the angels on your central panel using the photo as a guide to
placement. Once you are happy with the arrangement and colour
combination, fuse each shape in place. Do *not* put them too close to the
edge, as 1in (2.5cm) will be cut off very shortly. You can either sew a hand
or machine blanket stitch. I often combine hand and machine sewing in my
work, using quilting thread or two strands of embroidery thread. At this stage
do *not* embellish or add buttons. Trim the square to 16½in (42cm).

4 Cut four 16½in (42cm) lengths of wide ric-rac and pin them around the raw edges of the centre panel. The ric-rac should be a ¼in (6mm) from the edge of the central panel so you will need to sew halfway on to the ric-rac, so only little half moons will show (see the diagram on page 99). You could use lace instead of ric-rac.

Quick Tip...
Ric-racs come in different widths but what is important here is that you only sew a ¼in (6mm) seam when attaching them.

Border 1

5 The first border is very simple – see picture below. First cut out two 1½in (3.8cm) wide strips across the width of fabric, cutting two 16½in (42cm) long and another two 18½in (47cm) long. Sew the shorter ones on the top and bottom of the central panel and the longer strips to the sides, stitching on the same line of sewing you did for the ric-rac. Press, trim and check the size – it should measure 18½in (47cm) square.

Border 2

6 This is the folded Flying Geese border (see picture below), which is nice and easy and will make you feel like a real patchworker! From the lighter fabrics cut seventy-two squares each 2½in x 2½in (6.3cm x 6.3cm) and thirty-six rectangles each 4½in x 2½in (11.4cm x 6.3cm). The squares can be the same fabric or a mixture of one colour, but the 'geese', the rectangles, will look better in mixed fabrics but of the same colour.

7 Fold one rectangle, wrong sides together. Put the folded rectangle on to the right side of one of the squares, matching all raw edges in one corner. Place the other square on top, right sides together. Sew with a ¼in (6mm) seam along the side edge, which should incorporate the fold of the rectangle (see diagram on page 10).

8 Unfold the fabrics so that the two green squares lie flat and the edges of the rectangle are folded at a 45-degree angle. To do this, put your fingers between the layers of the rectangle fabric and push down on the fold until it lies directly on top of the seam that you have just sewn. Press the seam open, flattening it on the wrong side into a tiny triangle at the top. The tip of this triangle will be your sewing guide when you join the Flying Geese together.

9 Repeat for the remaining rectangles and squares to yield thirty-six folded Flying Geese units. Join units together in four strips of nine, with the geese all pointing in the same direction.

10 Join a strip of Flying Geese units to the top and bottom edges of the centre panel and press the seams towards Border 1. Now join a 4½in (11.4cm) square to each end of the remaining Flying Geese strips and then join these strips to the left and right edges of the centre panel. Press the seams towards Border 1.

Quick Tip...
If I can't get quite the right colour of ric-rac braid, I tone it down or up by embroidering on it – in this quilt I used French knots but you could use seed beads or other embroidery stitches.

11 Referring to the photograph on the previous page as a guide, fuse the flowers on to the corner blocks and blanket stitch (see page 102) around their raw edges as before. A detail of this quilting is shown here. Your quilt should now measure 26½in (67.3cm) square.

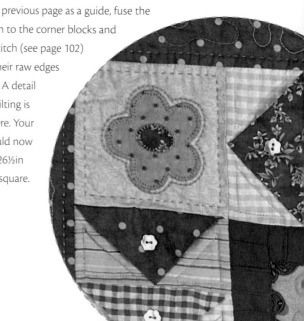

Border 3

12 This border could showcase a beautiful fabric: I choose plain dots but large florals also work really well. Start by cutting four strips 5½in (14cm) across the width of your fabric. Cut two strips 5½in x 26½in (14cm x 67.3cm) and sew them to the top and bottom edges of the quilt centre. Cut the remaining two strips to 36½in (92.7cm) and sew them to the left and right edges of the quilt centre. Your quilt should now measure 36½in (92.7cm) square. The ric-rac is sewn in place later.

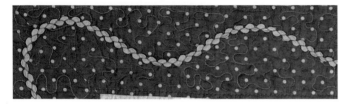

Border 4

13 This is nice and easy with 3½in (8.9cm) squares all joined together neatly in a row. Use the fabrics that already exist in the quilt plus others from your stash that match. Start by cutting and laying out fifty-two squares, in two rows of twelve squares and two rows of fourteen squares. Spread the light, medium and dark values around, and mix and match the size and colour of the prints. When you are happy with their placement, stitch the squares together in strips.

14 Join the two strips of twelve squares to the top and bottom edges of the quilt top and press the seams away from the quilt centre. Then join the two rows of fourteen squares to the left and right edges of the quilt top and press the seams away from the quilt centre.

Quick Tip . . .
I used the pattern of the large flower as a quilting template for some of the plainer squares, which I felt needed a 'lift'.

Border 5

15 The final border could be any measurement you like to make up the required size, but I cut mine 5½in (14cm) wide. Measure through the centre of the quilt to get a measurement for the width and cut two of your strips this length. Sew them to the top and the bottom of the quilt. Now measure through the centre of the quilt vertically to get the length of your final border and sew these strips to each side of the quilt. Press all seams.

16 Using fusible webbing and blanket stitch, appliqué the set of three flowers into each corner to finish this border, overlapping them if you wish, to create an attractive look.

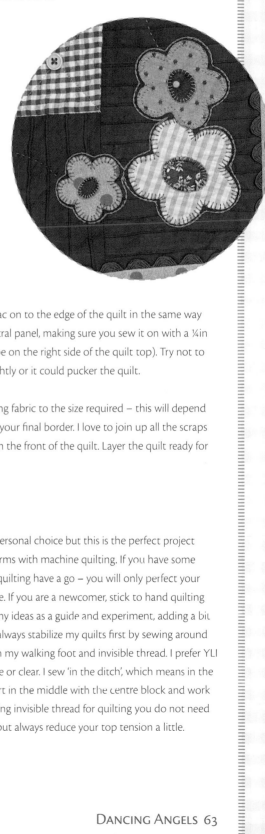

Ric-rac edge

17 Place the ric-rac on to the edge of the quilt in the same way as for the central panel, making sure you sew it on with a ¼in (6mm) seam, (this will be on the right side of the quilt top). Try not to put the braid on too tightly or it could pucker the quilt.

18 Cut the backing fabric to the size required – this will depend on the size of your final border. I love to join up all the scraps that I have left over from the front of the quilt. Layer the quilt ready for quilting – see page 100.

Quilting

19 Quilting is a personal choice but this is the perfect project to come to terms with machine quilting. If you have some experience in machine quilting have a go – you will only perfect your technique if you practise. If you are a newcomer, stick to hand quilting initially. You could use my ideas as a guide and experiment, adding a bit of 'you' into the quilt. I always stabilize my quilts first by sewing around all the straight lines with my walking foot and invisible thread. I prefer YLI invisible thread in smoke or clear. I sew 'in the ditch', which means in the middle of the seam. Start in the middle with the centre block and work your way out. When using invisible thread for quilting you do not need to use it in the bobbin but always reduce your top tension a little.

20 *Centre panel:* Free machine around all the angels and flower shapes using invisible thread, or the same colour thread as the background fabric. If you are quilting by hand, sew around all the angels with a small, neat running stitch. See page 100 for quilting: if this gets you all excited you can sew on the buttons now and decorate the clothing for the centre panel.

21 *Border 1:* I used a pin-tuck fabric that did not require quilting, but if your fabric is plain then I suggest a freehand wiggly line. I would draw it in first with a fine pencil.

22 *Border 2:* using matching thread, quilt using your ¼in (6mm) machine foot, echoing the Flying Geese shapes and sewing ¼in (6mm) from the edge of the triangles.

23 *Border 3:* on this border I used a template to mark the position for the ric-rac. Enlarge the templates on page 113 by 200% and then trace the curves on to template plastic or thin cardboard and cut out on the lines. Mark lightly in case you need to adjust the line. Lay the template on the edge of Border 3, as indicated on the pattern, and mark the lines for the ric-rac with your pencil. Lay the ric-rac over the traced lines and pin or tack (baste) to hold. Sew on the ric-rac using three strands of embroidery thread or a single-stranded thread, into the wadding but not right through to the back (see diagram on page 99).

24 *Border 4: w*ith matching thread sew a cross in each square (see picture below), either by eye or by marking a cross with a pencil and ruler or even masking tape. I finished off by sewing a button in the centre of each cross. If you have a particularly plain square, quilt a flower in it using the pattern for the appliqué flowers.

25 *Border 5:* Quilt around the flowers. Sew a large freehand wiggly line – you can use the templates you made before as a guide but they will need a bit of tweaking.

Binding and finishing off

26 Bind the quilt using 2¾in (7cm) wide binding, following the instructions on page 101. Now adorn your quilt by sewing on the rest of your buttons (or even to cover up little mistakes?). Titivate the angels with beads and hairbands, blusher, lippy – you know the sort of thing (see Quick Tip below). Sew on a label with your name, date and town (see page 101) and then hang the quilt, give it away or snuggle under it.

> *Quick Tip...*
> I use Pigma permanent pens for drawing faces. They are available in various colours and with fine and medium tips. They are also useful for signing quilts. They do not fade so the effects last forever.

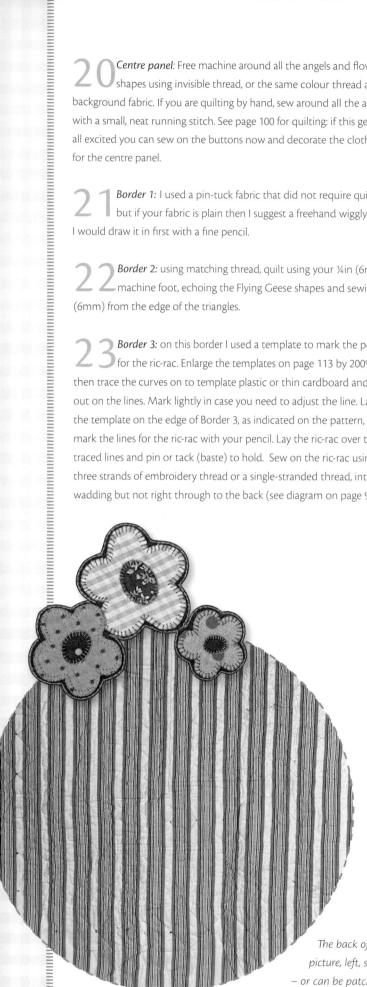

The back of your quilt can be from a single fabric – the picture, left, shows the back of the Dancing Angels quilt – or can be patched from various fabrics used in the quilt.

Anja and Ron

This gorgeous doll and her sweet little friend is great fun to make and dress – change the colours to suit what fabrics you have available. Her hair is made with piping cord, which after tea dyeing and drying, opens out to reveals a modern, highlighted look.

Finished size: 15in x 10¼in (38cm x 26cm) approx
Techniques: Using templates (page 96) ● Tea dyeing (page 96) ● Freezer paper (page 96) ● Ric-rac (page 99)

Ingredients

- Fat quarter of tea-dyed calico (see step 1)
- Cotton piping cord (tea dyed) 3yd (3m)
- Fabric for skirt 10in x 24in (25.4cm x (61cm)
- Fabric for pantaloons 8in x 12in (20.3cm x 30.5cm)
- Felt for jacket 10in (25.4cm) square
- Fat quarter of fabric for wings
- White felt for Ron 6in (15.3cm) square
- Bag of stuffing
- Cotton wadding (batting) for wing stuffing 10in x 8in (25.4cm x 20.3cm)
- Thin elastic for skirt and pantaloons
- Pigma permanent pens for drawing the face
- Decorative buttons – flower and small heart
- Glue gun
- Two skeins of cotton à broder for knitting a scarf

1 Refer to page 96 for using freezer paper and the tea-dyeing technique to be used on the calico and piping cord. Enlarge all the templates on page 114 by 200% on a photocopier to bring them up to full size ready for use.

Making the doll

2 Trace the templates for the body, arm and leg on to freezer paper. If you do not have freezer paper then ordinary paper will do. Fold the fat quarter of tea-dyed calico in half and either iron the templates on to it if using freezer paper, or pin them on. If you are not using freezer paper, draw around each template with a fine pencil. You will need to draw one body, two arms and two legs. Leave a ½in (1.3cm) gap between each template.

3 Using matching thread, sew the body and arms close to the edge of the freezer pattern or on the marked line, with a very small stitch – I use a number 2 on my Bernina. Do not sew across any openings, as indicated on the patterns for body, arm and leg, but do reinforce each end of the openings. If your calico has a very open weave, sew around the hands twice. Cut out the pattern pieces with a *scant* ¼in (6mm) seam (too big a seam and you will not be able to turn the arms the right way out).

4 Turn the body right way out. Turn the arms the right way out by putting a large straw into the arm to the end, then push a blunt stick down into the end of the straw on top of the fabric, lick your fingers and gently push the arm over the stick. This is sometimes tricky to start with but with a bit of coaxing it works a treat. Make the legs in the same way as the body and arms but with a nice fabric – horizontal stripes work well.

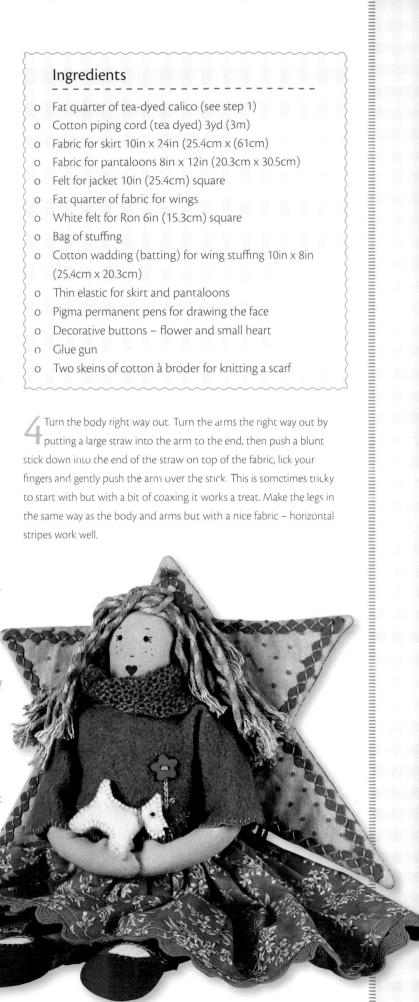

Stuffing the doll

5 Turn the body the right way out and stuff using small balls of stuffing the size of a walnut. The neck and shoulders must be well stuffed and firm to hold the head, and once they are done you can continue to stuff the body. Leave the gap along the bottom open to accommodate the legs.

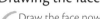

Quick Tip...
I find a chop-stick very useful for stuffing but you could also use blunt knitting needles or the handle of a small wooden spoon.

Drawing the face

6 Draw the face now (so if you get it wrong you can turn the body over and try on the other side!). Practise on a piece of calico first. Using the pattern as a guide, draw on the face with permanent pens readily available form patchwork shops (don't use the sort that bleed). Less is more: try not to have great big fat lips and huge eyelashes – not a good look at the best of times!

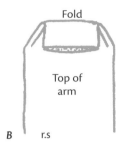

Stuffing legs and arms

7 The legs and arms are always a bit tricky to stuff so use very small balls of stuffing the size of peas: if you put too much in at once you will get the lumpy effect of varicose veins or worse! Don't use too much force as this may split the seams and you will have to start again. Stuff the arms firmly but the legs should only be stuffed firmly to the knee and then gently up to 1in (2.5cm) from the top.

8 Once the legs are stuffed pin them to the front of the bottom opening, as shown in Fig 1. Sew them in place along this seam by hand. Put the legs down and sew again along the same seam, sewing into the back of the body and tucking in any stray stuffing, and even adding a bit more if necessary. If you find that one leg is longer than the other, adjust by ladder stitching the longer leg up a bit.

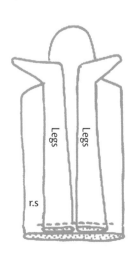

Fig 1 *Attaching the legs to the body*

9 Fold the sides of the top of the arms in (see Fig 2A), and then fold over the top (2B). Now sew the arms on to the shoulder of the body (see Fig 3).

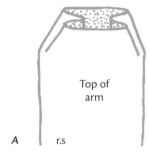

Fig 2 *Folding in the sides of the arms (A) and then folding over the top of the arm (B)*

Fig 3 *Attaching the arm to the body*

Hair

10 Cut up the tea-dyed piping cord into 8in (20.3cm) lengths. Lay them on to a piece of paper with a line marked through the centre (see Fig 4). Sew through the middle of the piping cord and paper, keeping all the cord tightly together so there are no gaps. Sew over this line two or three times and then tear off the paper. Unwind each strand of piping cord and the dyed effect will become evident. Using a glue gun, fix the hair on to the head. Try not to glue it dead flat – scrunch it up a little to give it some height.

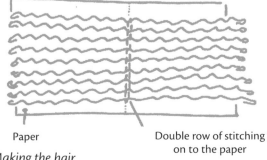

Paper   Double row of stitching on to the paper

Fig 4 *Making the hair*

Skirt

11 Cut out a rectangle 10in x 24in (25.4cm x 61cm) for the skirt, sew up the back seam and hem the bottom edge. Decorate the bottom edge of the hem with ric-rac. Turn the top over by ½in (1.3cm) and sew a chunky ¼in (6mm) seam from the folded edge to make a case for the elastic. Thread the elastic through the channel, fit the skirt on the doll, gather up the elastic and tie off.

Pantaloons

12 Fold the fabric for the pantaloons in half to 8in x 6in (20.3cm x 15.2cm). Using the pattern for the pantaloons cut out two, being careful to place the pattern on the fabric fold. Open out the shapes, place them right sides together and sew the two curved seams from 'a' to 'b' (see Fig 5). Snip the curved seam. Re-fold the pantaloons so the two curved seams sit on top of each other and sew the crotch seam, from 'c' to 'b' to 'c', as shown on Fig 6. Turn the top over to make a casing for the elastic and hem the bottom edge of each leg. The arrow on the pattern indicates the direction of the fabric grain.

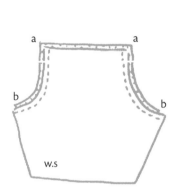

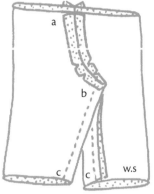

Fig 5 Sewing the pantaloon pieces together

Fig 6 Sewing the pantaloon crotch seam

Jacket

13 Fold a 10in (25.4cm) square of felt in half and half again. Place the jacket template on top of the felt, matching the folds, and cut out (see Fig 7). Open out the jacket and sew the under-arm seams. Decorate the edges with blanket stitch. Sew on a flower button and add a backstitch stem and lazy daisy stitches for two leaves (see page 103).

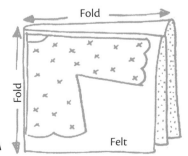

Fig 7 Placing the jacket pattern on the folded felt (A) and sewing up the underarm seams (B)

Shoes

14 Using the pattern cut the shoes out of felt. Cut one of each *in reverse*: this won't be a problem if you use felt but if you use another fabric (with a right side and wrong side) it is very important. Place the back and front of the shoe, rights side together. Sew from 'A' to 'B', and then turn right way out. Blanket stitch the top and front edges.

Wings

15 Cut two rectangles 10in x 8in (25.4cm x 20.3cm) out of wing fabric and a piece of wadding (batting) the same size. Place the rectangles right sides together and iron on the freezer paper wing template. Place the wadding to the back of the rectangles. Sew close to the line of the template through all layers all the way around. Cut the wings out ¼in (6mm) from the edge. Snip into the corners and snip off the points. Cut a slit in the top layer of the wings, as indicated on the pattern. Turn the right way out. Sew the ric rac in place ¼in (6mm) in from the edge using the stitch shown on page 99. Sew a decorative running stitch around the outside edge of the wings in contrasting thread. Glue the wings to the top of her shoulders, on the back.

Scarf

16 Finish Anja by knitting a scarf using two skeins of cotton à broder, unwound and rolled into a ball (or matching crochet thread). Cast on forty stitches on to size 5 needles and knitting loosely, knit two rows and then cast off a stitch at each end of the next and every alternate row until you have two stitches left, and then cast off.

Ron

17 How could we leave sweet little Ron to last? Cut the pattern out in cream felt. Fold the gusset in half and sew with a blanket stitch to one side of the body, 'A' to 'B'. Sew the other side of the gusset to the other body. Sew the two bodies together leaving a small gap for stuffing. Stuff firmly and then sew the gap closed. Sew on two small beads for eyes, and add a small piece of ribbon for a collar. Snuggle Ron in Anja's arms and sew in place.

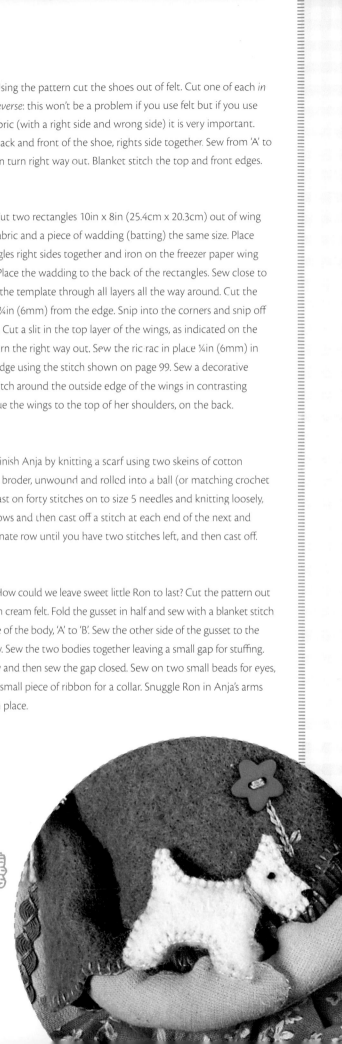

Quilter's Collection

Sewing rolls and pincushions are what I love making most and I've made hundreds! I feel very loyal to them all and each one has a different use. I have sewing rolls with embroidery threads in, one for hand quilting, one for making dolls and bears, an everyday one that I take to work-shops and one for taking on holidays. I also have pincushions in almost every room, in every drawer and on most work surfaces – now you thought you had a problem! This sewing roll features crazy patchwork created with an easy strip and flip technique, while the pincushion, really just two triangles sewn together, has great charm. Mmm. . . now what shall I use these lovely ones for?

The problem with my loyalty to my sewing rolls and pincushions is that I am sometimes very confused as to what's in what and where my favourite little tools are. So I end up taking them all with me wherever I go and subsequently can't find a thing – which is just not conducive to an organized life!

This elegant sewing roll and pincushion are not only really useful but great fun to make and are the perfect excuse to use up any oddments of braids and trims you might have.

French Fancy Sewing Roll

This is an easy and useful sewing roll *and* it's the perfect excuse to use up some of your stash of ribbons and braids – if not, time to go shopping! I avoided traditional patchwork fabrics and gave it a French feel by scouring charity (thrift) shops for linens and red checks.

Finished size: 10in x 17in (25.4cm x 43.2cm)
Techniques: Crazy stitch and flip (page 98) • Appliqué (page 98) • Ric-rac (page 99) • Binding (page 101)

Ingredients

- o Fat quarter of plain linen for pockets
- o Red check fabric for lining 20in x 10in (50.8cm x 25.4cm)
- o Calico 20in x 10in (50.8cm x 25.4cm)
- o Red polka dot fabric for middle pocket 7in x 10in (17.8cm x 25.4cm)
- o Scraps of linen-type cloth (see Quick Tip below)
- o Thin cotton wadding (batting) 20in x 10in (50.8cm x 25.4cm)
- o Binding fabric 60in (152.5cm)
- o Assortment of laces, braids, ric-rac and tapes
- o Zip (zipper) to match embroidery 10in (25.4cm) long
- o D-ring
- o Buttons and charms to decorate
- o Popper fastener
- o Tape 2in (5cm) wide x 6in (15.3cm) long (or fabric strip)

Quick Tip...
The linen-type cloth used for this sewing roll could include old French tea towels, vintage fabrics, old embroidery cloths and antimacassars (I love that word!).

Making the crazy patchwork panel

1 Using the 20in x 10in (50.8cm x 25.4cm) calico as a foundation, crazy piece, using the stitch and flip technique on page 98. Once finished, decorate the crazy piece with braids and ribbons and lace. Spray adhere or pin the 20in x 10in (50.8cm x 25.4cm) piece of wadding to the wrong side of the 20in x 10in (50.8cm x 25.4cm) rectangle of lining fabric. Put aside for the moment.

Making the zip pocket

2 Cut two pieces of linen 4in x 10in (10.2cm x 25.4cm) and one 8in x 10in (20.3cm x 25.4cm). Fold these in half wrong sides together so they measure 2in x 10in (5.1cm x 25.4cm) and 4in x 10in (10.2cm x 25.4cm) respectively. On the folded edges, sew on a piece of plain tape or ribbon (Fig 1A). Take the smaller piece and put the zipper under the folded edge, which will be on the right-hand side, and secure with pins. The zipper pull should be at the top (but in my project it's at the bottom, whoops!). Using thread that matches your tape or ribbon and the zipper foot on your sewing machine, sew close to the zip teeth. You may have to undo the zip to allow the machine foot to pass the zipper pull. Sew another line ¼in (6mm) from the first (Fig 1B). Place the other folded piece on the right-hand side of the zip, making sure the folded pieces all line up. Secure with a pin and sew close to the teeth of the zip. Sew another line ¼in (6mm) away from the first line (Fig 1C).

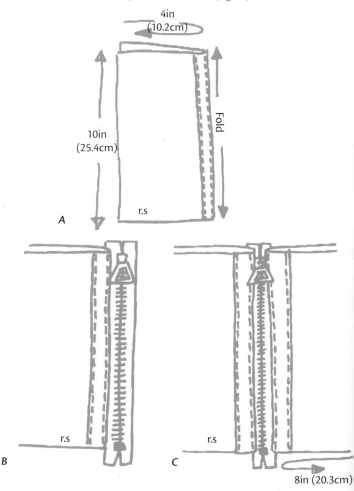

Fig 1 *The three stages in making the zip pocket (A, B and C)*

Exterior view of the sewing roll, showing the crazy patchwork and the various braids and tapes decorating the seams.

Zip pocket

Ruler pocket

Middle pocket

Folded pocket

Interior layout of the sewing roll, showing the pockets, accessories and decorations.

3 Place this pocket on to the left-hand side of the prepared lining, with the wrong side of the pocket to the right side of the lining (see Fig 2 and also the detail picture on the previous page). Make sure the zipper pull is at the *top* and that the shorter side of the pocket is to the left. Pin in place. Attach the pocket to the lining by sewing a piece of tape or ribbon on to the right-hand side of the pocket.

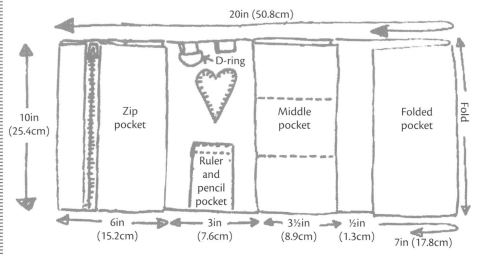

20in (50.8cm)

D-ring

Zip pocket

Middle pocket

Folded pocket

Fold

10in (25.4cm)

Ruler and pencil pocket

6in (15.2cm)   3in (7.6cm)   3½in (8.9cm)   ½in (1.3cm)

7in (17.8cm)

Fig 2 *Position of the pockets on the inside of the sewing roll*

Quick Tip...
Check out scrapbooking stores for great haberdashery, especially for collections of laces, braids, ric-rac and tapes.

Making the middle pocket

4 Cut a contrasting piece of fabric 7in x 10in (17.8cm x 25.4cm) – I used a red polka dot. Fold it in half to 3½in x 10in (8.9cm x 25.4cm). Decorate the folded end with ribbon or tape. Divide this pocket into 3¼in (8.25cm) and then 3½in (8.9cm) and then 3¼in (8.25cm) and mark these divisions with a pin or a fine pencil line. Measure a 3in (7.6cm) gap between the zip pocket and where the middle pocket will be and mark with a pin (see Fig 2).

Place the folded end of the middle pocket on the mark. Pin in place. Sew the divisions through to the lining fabric. Sew on a ribbon or tape to cover the raw ends of the pocket.

Making the ruler and pencil pocket

5 I managed to find a piece of webbing tape 2in (5cm) wide for this pocket but you could use a strip of linen. Decorate the tape with ribbon and little buttons. Fold over the top twice and hem. Place the pocket on to the lining between the two other pockets and sew in place.

The middle pocket (see picture above) can be embellished with sewing-themed charms. The finished sewing roll (see picture right) is kept all neat and tidy by a length of decorative tape wound around the folded roll and then around a large button.

6 Copy the template given in Fig 3 (it is full size). The heart will be
a needle catcher. Trace the heart on to non-sew lightweight
interfacing. Pin a piece of fabric slightly larger than the heart to the
interfacing, wrong sides together. Sew on the marked line all the way
around. Cut out the heart close to the stitching line. Cut a slit in the
interfacing, turn the right way out and ladder
stitch in place (see page 103). Cut a
4in (10.2cm) piece of ribbon or
tape, fold in half and pin the
raw ends to the top of the 3in
(7.6cm) wide gap. You can
attach your keys or a bag
charm to this. I made
another with a D-ring
attached for the same
purpose.

Heart
template

Fig 3 *Heart template (actual
size), with seams allowed for*

Assembling the roll

7 Put the crazy patchwork panel on top of the
lining, right sides together and sew the right-hand
seam. Open out and press the seam allowances to one
side. Fold the crazy panel back and press. Make sure the
crazy panel and the lining all match and trim if necessary.
Pin or tack (baste) the raw edges. From the lining side, fold
over 3½in (8.9cm) on the right-hand side to make the final pocket.
Pin in place.

8 Bind the three raw edges of the sewing roll with 1¾in (4.4cm)
wide single binding (double will be too bulky) – see page 101 for
binding instructions. Cut a length of tape or ribbon 16in (40.6cm)
long and attach it to the centre of the left-hand side edge of the
crazy patchwork side and sew a large button on top. Fold over the
other raw end and sew a smaller button on each side. This tape will
wrap around the roll and fasten off around the button – see picture on
opposite page.

9 Now use your imagination and decorate the sewing
roll with a little embroidery and the odd button and
charm. I sewed a large popper on the right-hand side
pocket to keep it closed and added some heart
buttons to the ruler pocket. I also made a button pull
for the zip – just put some embroidery thread into the
hole of the zipper pull, thread on some small buttons
or beads and tie them off at the end.

Quick Tip...
If I think a space is too bland
and needs filling, I use a
template from the pattern
and add a bit of stitching or
a button. The detail picture,
left, shows the heart shape
from the pincushion.

Heart Pincushion

This useful pincushion looks complicated but it's really only two triangles sewn together. I used the same fabrics as the sewing roll and decorated the pincushion with buttons and braid for a rustic look.

Ingredients

o   Main fabric 8in (20.3cm) square
o   Fabric for pocket 4in (10.2cm) square
o   Five different braids, ribbons, ric-rac or lace, each about 6in (15.2cm) long
o   Large handful of stuffing
o   Ribbon or tape to decorate pocket 10in (25.4cm)
o   Ribbon or tape for bow 10in (25.4cm)
o   Ric-rac or ready-made piping for outside edge 20in (50.8cm) long

1 Cut the 8in (20.3cm) square of fabric in half diagonally. Fold the 4in (10.2cm) square in half diagonally and press (see Fig 1A). Decorate one half of the 8in (20.3cm) square on the right side with ribbons, lace and braids (Fig 1B). Pin first to arrange the ribbons nicely and then sew them in place.

2 Decorate the top folded edge of the smaller triangle with braid, ribbon or lace. Place this folded triangle on to the other half of the 8in (20.3cm) square and tack (baste) in place. This now acts as a pocket. Tack piping cord or ric-rac to the right side of the two shorter edges of one of the pocketed triangles – see picture below.

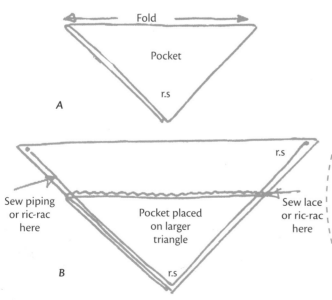

Fig 1 *Folding the 10in (25.4cm) square into a triangle to make the pocket (A) and then placing this triangle on to the larger triangle (B). The picture, right, shows the finished pocket*

3 Place both triangles right sides together and sew all the way around leaving a 3in (7.6cm) opening in the middle of the long edge (see Fig 2 below). At each end of the longer side, squash the side seam on to the top seam ('sugar bagging') and sew 1in (2.5cm) in from the point (see Fig 3). Trim off the points.

Quick Tip. . .
You could stuff the pincushion with sawdust bought from a pet store. Better still, put some lavender flowers or spices in with the stuffing to give a lovely waft of smells every time you use the pincushion.

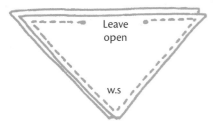

Fig 2 Sewing the triangles together

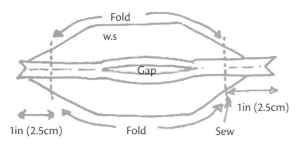

Fig 3 'Sugar bagging' both ends of the triangles

4 Turn the right way out and stuff firmly, but do not stuff into the points. Close the opening with ladder stitching (see page 103). Fold over both 'points' so they butt up to each other and ladder stitch them together (see picture below, right). To finish, use a piece of ribbon or tape to tie a bow through the top of the heart.

This detail picture, right, shows the top of the pincushion, where the two triangles are sewn together. Disguise the join with some tape tied around the junction in a bow.

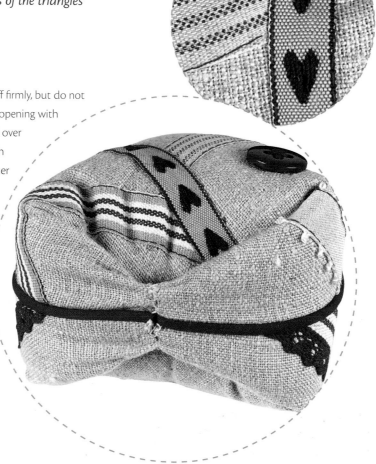

Crazy But Cosy

This crazy patchwork throw uses rich, warm colours and is so easy to make – just one crazy patchwork block, with the fabrics shuffled into different positions in each of the nine blocks. Add some sashing and a border and voila! Very little accuracy is needed, just a nice collection of fabrics that 'go' with each other in colour and tone. I used extra soft minkie fabric for a backing but fleece would do just as well. Using minkie or fleece means that you do not need to use any wadding. After you have made the throw you will have a block left over, which is ideal for a cushion – see the picture on page 80.

While you're snuggling up on the sofa under the cosy throw, you could also make a pair of soft slippers, or two – perfect for a chilly winter evening. The slippers are intended to be a loose fit but the sizes are easy to change – see page 81 for the slipper instructions.

If you're mad about fabrics then you will surely have a supply of thicker materials, such as velvets, brocades, corduroys and denim, which would be perfect for this throw – or it'll be an excuse to go out and buy some! A pair of slippers will make a cosy evening even more comfortable.

Cosy Crazy Throw

This method of crazy quilting is fun, easy and a great fat quarter user-upper. If you want the quilt larger just use multiples of five more fat quarters. My layout for the throw is shown overleaf. After you have made the throw you can use the spare block for a cushion (see picture below and page 80).

Finished size: 48in (122cm) square
Techniques: Using templates (page 96) ● Freezer paper (page 96) ● Crazy stitch and flip (page 98) ● Borders (page 99) ● Binding (page 101)

Ingredients

- o Collection of ten fat quarter fabrics, such as velvets, brocades, corduroys and denim (this includes border)
- o Sashing fabric, a thin quarter
- o Backing fabric (fleece or minkie) 52in (132cm) square
- o Binding fabric ½yd (0.5m)
- o Freezer paper 1yd (1m)
- o Embroidery or wool threads for quilting

1 Start by enlarging the crazy block template from page 115 by 200% on a photocopier. Trace the template from your photocopy on to freezer paper, twice. Do remember to transfer the numbers of each piece. *Do not cut out.* Don't worry if you do not have any freezer paper, just use ordinary paper and pin it to the fabric.

2 Prepare your fabrics by pressing them all and stacking them neatly on top of each other, *right sides facing up*. Stack two sets of five, and iron a freezer paper pattern on the top layer of each stack. With a large rotary cutter or large scissors cut the outside square first and then cut the individual sections. This might be a bit tricky if your fabrics are thick but accurate cutting isn't needed at this stage, so just do your best. *Do not shuffle them about, keep them in the right sequence, and stack as a square.* Peel off the freezer paper from the top layer and place it on the bottom of the pile so you know which number this stack is.

Preparing your fabric stacks

3 Ignore Stack 1. Put the top fabric from Stack 2 to the bottom of the stack. In Stack 3 put the top fabric to the bottom and then the second fabric to the bottom. In Stack 4 put the top fabric to the bottom, then the second and then the third. In Stack 5 put the top fabric to the bottom, then the second, then the third and then the fourth. *Very important: each fabric must be moved individually to the bottom of each stack.*

4 Pop the cut-up square on to a tray, as it is, and take it with you to your sewing machine. Take a piece of fabric from the top of Stack 1 and Stack 2 and sew right sides together with a ¼in (6mm) seam. You do not need to be too accurate. Add to this a piece from Stack 3, and then add a piece from Stack 4 and finally a piece from Stack 5. The first block is complete (see example below). Leave to one side for pressing later. Continue sewing all the other blocks.

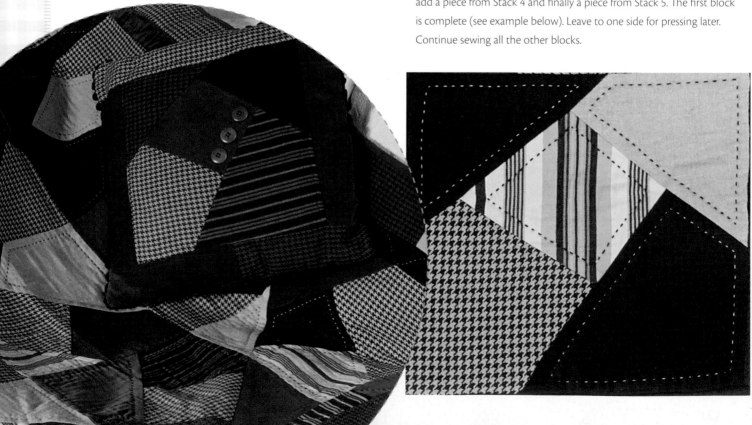

5 When you have sewn the two stacks of five you should end up with ten different blocks (one is the spare you can use for a cushion). Press them well and cut each individual block to 12½in (31.75cm) square exactly. Join these blocks together in rows of three, twisting and turning the blocks so no two fabrics touch each other – not that easy, but do your best. Sew with a consistent seam – a ¼in (6mm) might be too narrow with thicker fabrics. If the sewing machine seems to be having difficulty, pop in a new, larger needle.

Adding the border

6 You can add a narrow border before sewing on the wider outer border. Cut strips 2½in (6.3cm) wide and sew to the top and bottom of the throw first and then to the sides – see page 99.

7 For the wider border cut your remaining fabric into 6½in (16.5cm) strips and piece them together. This is done randomly. Cut a strip to fit along the top of the throw and one for the bottom, sew and press seams out. Now add the two side borders.

Layering

8 Pin your backing fabric to the carpet, wrong side facing you, smooth your wadding (if you are using any) and then your crazy pieced top. Pin all three layers together well, especially at the edges.

Quilting and binding

9 Using matching thread (if you are brave) or invisible thread, stabilize all the blocks by sewing in the ditch down and along all the rows and then, finally, around the outside edge. You will need your walking foot attachment on your machine to do this. Using chunky thread, embroider some or all of the lines on the crazy blocks and feel free to quilt in the border to your heart's content, perhaps in wavy lines. You could add buttons for embellishment if desired. Bind the quilt (see page 101) using a 2¾in (7cm) wide binding to accommodate the thicker fabric. To make a quick cushion from the spare block, see overleaf.

Quick Tip. . .
When using thicker fabrics it will be nearly impossible to quilt conventionally, so use a chunky needle and thread and sew neat, larger-than-normal stitches.

After you have made the throw you will notice that you have a spare block left over, which is ideal for making a cushion. I used the scraps from the fat quarters to make the cushion up to 18in (45.7cm). I put wadding on the back, quilted it and decorated it with some chunky buttons. I created a backing by patching scraps together – now that's what I call economic! – and added a wide ric-rac edging.

Cosy Slippers

Aren't these the sweetest little slippers? They are quick and easy to make from your fat quarter stash and can be made for summer or winter use. They take very little time and can be decorated with small amounts of ric-rac, braids and buttons. The patterns are given in two sizes, small and large, but are easy to adjust by photocopying.

1 Choose the size you require – small and large patterns are provided on page 116, to fit the following shoe sizes: Small = 3–4 (UK), 35–36 (Europe), 3½–4½ (US and Canada). Large = 6–7 (UK), 38½–40 (Europe), 6½–7½ (US and Canada). Enlarge the templates on page 116 by 200% on a photocopier and trace the patterns on to sheets of paper. Using your pattern pieces cut out from main fabric two soles (one in reverse) and two sides (one in reverse). From lining fabric cut out two soles (one in reverse) and two sides (one in reverse).

2 Sew the back seam, using a ¼in (6mm) seam allowance on the main fabric and a fraction larger on the lining fabric. Decorate the top edge by tacking (basting) on some ric-rac braid or piping, using the guide provided on the pattern.

3 If you like the tab effect at the back of the slipper, insert it now by cutting a piece of tape 6in (15.2cm) long and folding it in half wrong sides together. Pin the tape so that it covers the back seam, with the raw edges of the tape to the bottom of the seam. Sew it in place, stopping ¼in (6mm) from the top, sewing across the tape and continuing down to the bottom.

4 Pin the sole in place by matching the centre of the slipper top with the notch on the sole. Do the same with the back seam. Pin well, easing the slipper top on to the sole, and then sew. Do the same with the lining, but leave a gap along the side seam for turning. Remember the lining seam allowance will be a fraction larger than ¼in (6mm). Trim seam allowances if necessary.

5 Turn the slipper inside out and put the lining slipper inside it, right way out. Right sides should now be touching. Match the back seams and pin all around the opening. Sew on the tacking lines of the ric-rac or a ¼in (6mm) seam allowance. Trim the seams and snip the

centre front of the opening. Turn right way out via the opening in the lining side. Sew the opening in the lining closed. Push the lining into the slipper. Sew ¼in (6mm) in from the top edge by machine or hand – this is for decoration and to keep the lining in place. Decorate the slipper with a button or a ric-rac flower, or both!

Making a ric-rac flower

6 Cut a piece of ric-rac 6in (15.2cm) long. Sew a gathering stitch through the middle of the ric-rac and pull it up tight. Overlap the raw ends to the back of the flower and fasten off. Attach the flower to the slipper by sewing a button in the middle. Make a second flower for the other slipper. Now isn't that nice!

All Things Christmas

Christmas is a very special time in our house and I put a lot of time and effort into creating a warm and cosy festive atmosphere, decorating everything with our makes. I never follow trends and hype: I prune the garden and use holly, ivy, tufts of lavender and evergreens to make garlands which are then decorated with little felt snowmen and red hearts. All of our chairs and sofas are bedecked with cosy, flannel-backed quilts and the walls are hung with quilts too. Bed posts have roomy Christmas stockings draped on them.

I can't wait to see how this Christmas quilt will look with all my others. It was such fun to make, and great for adding lots and lots of trimmings and embellishments – just go mad! There is also a bright festive garland on page 92 and both projects are perfect for you to create as they are easy, quick and timeless. Get started – Christmas isn't far away!

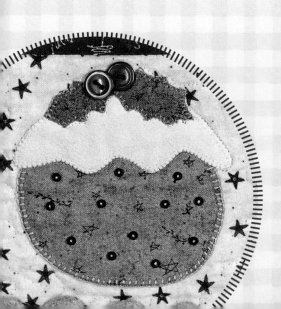

Christmas is the perfect opportunity to create a wonderful quilt that will allow you to practise some great techniques, and it is sure to be much admired and bring a cosy Christmas atmosphere to your home.

Sew a Row of Christmas Quilt

This is such a lovely quilt, which could also be a wall hanging. It has it all – appliqué, foundation piecing, stitch and flip and fast piecing. To create wall space for my festive quilts I take down pictures especially for the holiday period, which at least gets me dusting!

Band 1 Twinkle, twinkle little star. . .

1 This block is constructed using a fast piecing technique, requiring *accurate* cutting and sewing. It's a bit of a challenge, but together we can do it! To make the large star block, make a cardboard or plastic template 2⅞in (7.3cm) square. Draw on all the sewing lines as in Fig 1. Cut a *rough* rectangle 4in x 8in (10.1cm x 20.3cm) out of your star fabric and sky fabric and iron these two, right sides together. Mark on the lighter side of the fabric (the star side) the template you've just made, twice, using a fine pencil (see Fig 2). Draw in all the sewing lines.

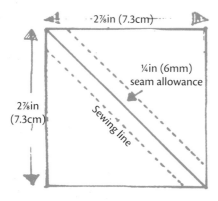

Fig 1 For the large star block, make a template 2⅞in (7.3cm) square and mark lines as shown here

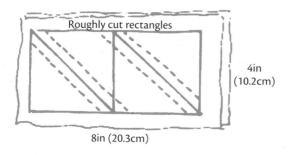

Fig 2 Marking the star and sky fabric twice with the template

Finished size: 44½in x 37½in (113cm x 95.2cm)
The finished size of the bands is of 27½in x 5½in (69.8cm x 14cm), except Band 1 which is 6½in (16.5cm) high
Techniques: Using templates (page 96) ● Foundation piecing (page 97) ● Appliqué (page 98) ● Stitch and flip (page 98) ● Ric-rac (page 99) ● Borders (page 99) ● Binding (page 101)

Ingredients

- Blue fabric for sky ½yd (0.5m)
- One fat quarter of fabric for yellow stars
- One fat quarter for Christmas trees background
- Five fat eighths of green fabric (or scraps) for trees
- One fat eighth of brown fabric for tree trunks
- Fabric for background to garland 6in x 30in (15.2cm x 76.2cm)
- Fabric scraps each 4in (10.2cm) square for mitten, gingerbread, snowman, holly, bell, candy cane, Father Christmas, angels and Rudolph
- Scraps for flying angels, trees and sleigh each 6in x 4in (15.2cm x 10.2cm)
- One fat quarter of fabric for background to presents and Christmas pudding
- Fabric for sashing ½yd (0.5m)
- Fabric for borders ½yd (0.5m)
- Backing fabric 1¼yd (1.25m)
- Wadding (batting) 1¼yd (1.25m)
- Binding fabric 4¼yd (4m) of 2¾in (7cm) wide
- Ric-rac braid, 1yd (1m) each in cream and green, plus a colour to match the present row
- Tape to match the garland row 1yd (1m)
- Four small bells and five tiny bells for angel's hair
- Decorative buttons:
  two small buttons for gingerbread;
  three small red buttons for star and holly berries;
  two small red heart buttons for Rudolf;
  one carrot button
- Twelve small black beads for eyes
- Beige felt for reindeers 3in (7.6cm) square
- Assorted ribbons and tapes to decorate trees and parcels
- Embroidery threads to match
- Fusible webbing ¼yd (0.25m)
- Scrap of sew-in interfacing
- Frayable green fabric for garland 3in x 45in (7.6cm x 114.3cm)

Band 1

Band 2

Band 3

Band 4

Band 5

Sashing

Border

This Christmas quilt looks complicated but is actually quite straight
forward. Just make the five bands, add some sashing and borders,
plus some appliqué decorations and masses of embellishments.

2 Pin the fabrics together in each half square. With small running stitches, sew along all four sewing lines, casting on and off within the squares if sewing by hand, but sewing off the edge if using your machine. Using a rotary cutter or sharp, long scissors, cut the outside squares first, then the diagonals. Press *lightly* to set the stitch, then open out your squares and press the light seam to the dark side. You have now made four half-square triangles.

3 Cut four 2½in (6.3cm) squares from sky fabric and one 2½in (6.3cm) square from star fabric. Using these and the four half-square triangles, arrange the large star block as shown in Fig 3. Sew the squares together in sets of three, and then sew the three strips together.

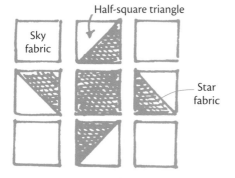

Fig 3 *Sewing the large star block together*

4 Using the same process but with a 1⅞in (4.9cm) square template (Fig 4), create the half-square triangles for the small star blocks – twenty-four in total to make six small star blocks. This time, cut four 1½in (3.8cm) squares from sky fabric and one 1½in (3.8cm) square from star fabric. Be careful when you construct the stars to ensure they are facing the right way: in the main photo you'll see I have a 'rogue' star or two – I didn't notice until it was all over!

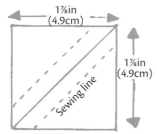

Fig 4 *For the small star block, make a template 1⅞in (4.9cm) square and mark lines as shown here*

5 Join the rows of stars together as follows (see Fig 5).
Row 1: sew a 3½in x 1½in (8.9cm x 3.8cm) strip of blue fabric to the top of a small star and a strip 3½in x 2½in (8.9cm x 6.3cm) to the bottom of that star.
Row 2: sew a 3½in x 2½in (8.9cm x 6.3cm) strip to the top of a small star and a 3½in x 1½in (8.9cm x 3.8cm) strip to the bottom.
Row 3: sew a 3½in (8.9cm) square to the bottom of a small star.
Row 4: this is the large star.
Row 5: sew a 3½in (8.9cm) square to the top of a small star.
Row 6: sew a 3½in (8.9cm) square to the bottom of a small star.
Row 7: sew a 3½in x 2½in (8.9cm x 6.3cm) strip on top of a small star and a 3½in x 1½in (8.9cm x 3.8cm) strip to the bottom.
Sew a 6½in x 2½in (16.5cm x 6.3cm) strip of sky fabric to the left side of Row 1. Sew a 6½in x 1½in (16.5cm x 3.8cm) strip of sky fabric to the right side of Row 7. Now sew all the rows together as shown in the diagram. When you have finished it should be 24½in (62.2cm) wide – if not adjust by giving it a good press or by adding or taking in a few seams.

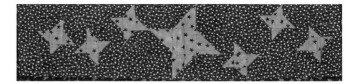

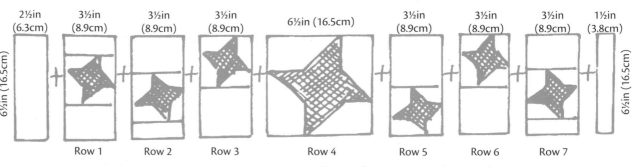

Fig 5 *Piecing the stars and strips together*

Band 2 Oh, Christmas tree...

6 This is a lovely little row of foundation-pieced Christmas trees. The background is all the same, but the trees are made using different fabrics. Once made and joined together they are all embellished and decorated – the best bit! There are five different trees.

Enlarge the five foundation piecing templates on page 117 by 200% on a photocopier and follow the foundation piecing instructions on page 97 to piece each tree. The foundation blocks are made in two pieces because otherwise the shapes will not flow in number sequence. Do not let this put you off because I have come up with a lovely idea for four of the trees: we will fast piece the tree trunk and its background all in one go and them cut it up into the right size for each tree. These four trees trunks will be the same but this won't matter.

From the tree trunk fabric cut one piece 1½in x 12in (3.8cm x 30.5cm). From the background fabric cut two pieces 2½in x 12in (6.3cm x 30.5cm). Sew these three strips together with the trunk fabric in the middle (see Fig 6). Press seams towards the middle. This strip of fabric can now be cut up into 2in (5cm) strips and added to the bottom edge of each foundation block, directly below each tree and on top of the marked trunks. The blocks would then have to be cut to size. The asterisks on the patterns show where to add the pieced tree trunks. When all five trees are made, sew them together in a row.

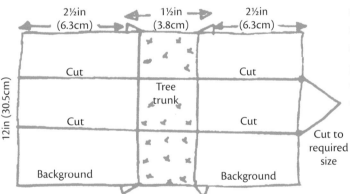

Fig 6 *Fast piecing tree trunks for trees 1, 2, 4 and 6*

Band 3 Deck the halls...

7 This is my favourite row, which has a garland hung with Christmas decorations. The row is appliquéd using a fusible webbing such as Bondaweb – so a pleasant relief after all that foundation piecing. Cut a strip of background fabric 27½in x 5½in (69.8cm x 14cm), making sure it is light in colour so the decorations show up well. Enlarge the templates on page 118 by 200% on a photocopier and use the patterns to cut your fabric pieces. Using fusible webbing and a hand or machine blanket stitch, appliqué the shapes on to the background, using the photograph as a guide to the positioning of the shapes. Make sure you do not put them in a straight line, as the garland needs to be wavy.

8 **Garland:** cut three strips 1in (2.5cm) wide in a green woven fabric (see Quick Tip below). Put the three strips on top of each other and sew down the middle of the length using matching thread. Snip up to the stitch line on each side, with snips ¼in (6mm) apart. Wet the garland and rub in some soap, agitating it with your hands, and then rinse and ring out. Dry using a tumble dryer if possible and the result should be a gorgeous shaggy garland. Pin the garland in position over the appliquéd shapes. This will be attached later with buttons when the quilting is done.

Quick Tip...
When choosing the fabric for the garland it's important to use an open weave or a woven fabric to achieve a rough and 'shaggy' look to the garland.

Band 4 We all love figgy pudding. . .

9 This band contains some appliqué, foundation piecing and a three-dimensional stocking that uses the flip and stitch technique.

Present One: referring to Fig 7 below, cut out a rectangle 4½in x 3½in (11.4cm x 8.9cm) in a present colour. From the background fabric cut: two 1½in (3.8cm) squares; two rectangles 1½in x 3½in (3.8cm x 8.9cm) and two rectangles 6½in x 1½in (16.5cm x 3.8cm). On the two small squares draw a diagonal line from corner to corner on the wrong side. Place one of these squares to the top left-hand corner of the present rectangle, right sides together. Sew on the diagonal line. Flip the half-square triangle back and press (see Fig 9). Cut off the triangles underneath. Repeat with the lower right-hand corner. Sew the two shorter rectangles to either side of the present block with a ¼in (6mm) seam, flip back and press. Sew the two longer rectangles to the top and bottom of the present block, flip back and press.

11 **Present Two:** referring to Fig 8 below, cut out a 3½in (8.9cm) square in a present colour. From the background fabric cut two 1½in (3.8cm) squares; two 1½in x 5½in (3.8cm x 14cm) rectangles and two 3½in x 1½in (8.9cm x 3.8cm) rectangles (see Fig 9). On the two small squares draw a diagonal line from corner to corner on the wrong side. Place one of these squares to the top left-hand corner of the present rectangle, right sides together and sew on the diagonal line. Flip the half-square triangle back and press. Cut off the triangles underneath. Repeat with the top right-hand corner. Now sew the two shorter rectangles to the top and bottom of the present block with a ¼in (6mm) seam, flip back and press. Sew the two longer rectangles to either side of the present block, flip back and press.

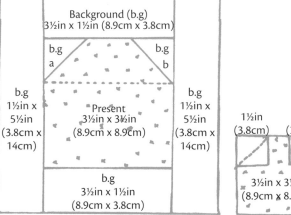

Fig 7 Patchwork pieces for Present One

Fig 8 Patchwork pieces for Present Two   *Fig 9 Making corner triang...*

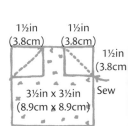

10 **Figgy pudding:** cut a 5½in (14cm) square in background fabric. Enlarge the template on page 118 by 200% and appliqué the pudding, topping and holly leaves on to the square using hand or machine blanket stitch (see page 102).

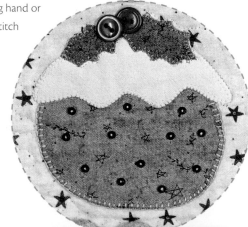

12 **Stocking:** the front of this three-dimensional stocking is constructed using 'stitch and flip' very similar to the crazy technique described on page 98. Cut a background square 5½in (14cm). Enlarge the template on page 118 by 200% and trace the pattern on to sew-in interfacing (see page 96). Collect small scraps from all the fabrics you've used: your aim is to cover the marked stocking on the interfacing. Start at the bottom and place a small piece of fabric on the stocking, with the right side facing you. Place another piece, right sides together, at a slight angle to provide interest, and stitch these two pieces on to the foundation. Flip the top fabric back and finger press. Place another piece of fabric on at an angle, right sides together, leaving no gaps and covering the line, and then sew and flip. Continue until the whole stocking is covered. *Do not cut out* the stocking shape from the interfacing.

13 Decorate the seams with decorative machine stitches or embroider it by hand when the stocking is finished. Press the stocking well and place a scrap of fabric, right sides together on top of the stocking. Turn over and using the marked line on the interfacing as a guide, sew all the way round leaving a gap on the side as indicated on the pattern. Trim to a scant ¼in (6mm) seam. Turn the right way out and slipstitch the opening closed. Decorate to your heart's content with embroidery, trims, buttons and beads. The stocking will be connected to its block later.

14 **Present Three:** referring to Fig 10, cut from the background fabric two rectangles 4½in x 1½in (11.4cm x 3.8cm) and two 3½in x 1½in (8.9cm x 3.8cm). Cut one rectangle in present fabric 2½in x 3½in (6.3cm x 8.9cm). Cut two pieces of thin ribbon 6in (15.2cm) long and one 3in (7.6cm) long. On the present rectangle pin the shorter piece of ribbon across at 'c' and 'd'. Pin the two longer pieces to 'a' and 'b'. Tuck the longer lengths of ribbon in so they do not get caught in your sewing. Sew the two smaller rectangles to either side of the present, flip back and press. Sew the two longer rectangles to the top and bottom of the present, flip back and press. Join all the blocks together as in the diagram.

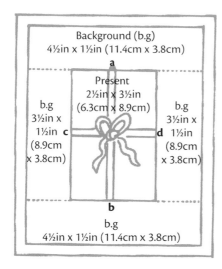

Fig 10 Patchwork pieces for Present Three

Band 5 Silent night. . .

15 Cut out a background rectangle 26½in x 5½in (67.3cm x 14cm). Enlarge all the templates on page 118 by 200% and use the patterns to appliqué the sleepy evening scene, using fusible webbing and a hand or machine blanket stitch. Use the photograph on page 85 to help you place the shapes. When you have finished the appliqué on this block, tack on the large white ric-rac to the bottom edge, so the humps of the braid are in line with the bottom edge, to resemble snow.

Adding the sashing

16 The sashing is cut 2½in (6.3cm) wide for a 2in (5cm) finished size. Cut across the width of the fabric, cutting accurately and pressing each piece of sashing well. These measurements all work well as long as the blocks measurements are correct, so adjust accordingly if you have any hiccups. All seam allowances are still ¼in (6mm). Some sashing may need to be joined. Cut six strips 27½in x 2½in (69.8cm x 6.3cm). Use these between each band and one on the top and the bottom. Cut two strips 38½in x 2½in (97.8cm x 6.3cm) and sew these in place on either side of the sewn bands.

Adding the border

17 Cut two strips 31½in x 3½in (80cm x 8.9cm) for the top and bottom borders. Sew them on nicely, pressing as you go. Cut two strips 44½in x 3½in (113cm x 8.9cm) and sew in place as the two side borders.

18 To adorn the borders of the quilt, enlarge the templates on page 119 by 200% and use the patterns, fusible webbing and a hand or machine blanket stitch to appliqué the two angels, the two trees, the star, the sleigh and the word 'Noel'. Refer to the photo on page 85 for placements.

Quick Tip . . .
Don't be tempted to embellish this quilt as you go: it's best to sew on all the goodies after you have layered up the quilt, as they will act as quilting and save you time.

Layering the quilt

19 Give the quilt a good tidy up, sewing in or cutting off loose ends and pressing. Cut the backing fabric 40in x 48in (101.6cm x 121.9cm), joining if necessary – I love to use up all the scraps that I have left over from the front. Cut out the wadding (batting) the same size as the backing and then refer to page 100 for layering instructions.

Quilting

20 Quilting is a personal choice and I happen to adore machine quilting, but I always mix in a bit of hand quilting too. What this quilt needs is for the backgrounds to be quilted so the characters stand out. It is the perfect project to practise machine quilting. So use my ideas as a guide and feel free to personalize. I always stabilize my quilts first by sewing around all the straight lines with my walking foot and invisible thread. I prefer YLI invisible thread in smoke or clear. I sew 'in the ditch', which means in the middle of the seam. Start in the middle with the centre block and work your way out. Remember that when using invisible thread you do not need to use it in the bobbin, but reduce your tension a little.

Adding embellishments

21 This is the fun but time-consuming bit, but once you start you just cannot stop!

Oh Christmas Tree: sew on a collection of trims, charms and buttons for the tree.s I appliquéd stars to the tree tops because I couldn't find the right button.

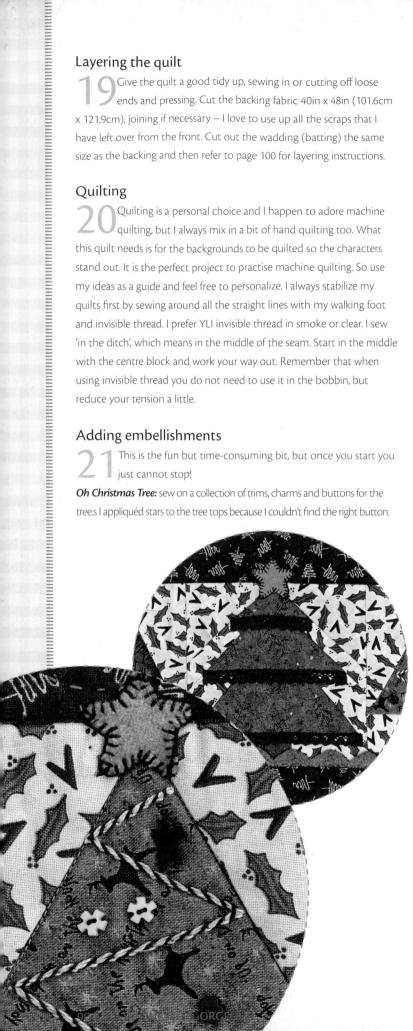

Deck the halls: I sewed on lots of little buttons to the gloves, snowman and gingerbread man. I embroidered crosses on the bell and veins on the holly leaves. I decorated the garland by attaching it to the quilt with little red bells.

We all love figgy pudding: sew red buttons on to the holly to represent berries and brown buttons on the pudding to represent raisins. Sew a button on the stocking block to hang up the stocking. Sew ribbon on to the parcels and tie a bow on the third parcel. You could also make a three-dimensional gift tag for the first present, using two pieces of felt blanket stitched together and embellished with a message.

Silent night: sew a bell to the end of Santa's hat and on Rudolf's neck. Embroider a cluster of French knots (see page 102) to Rudolph's head, a few freckles on his cheeks and backstitch his mouth. Sew a red button on for his nose. Sew a wooden button to the top of the tree or appliqué a star. Sew little bells on the angel's hair and buttons on her dress and the snowman's body. Sew beads on for the snowman's mouth and eyes. Sew pearly buttons for stars above the snowman's head.

Borders and sashing: sew star buttons on to top of the Christmas trees and little bells down the centres. Finally, the pretty angels have star buttons sewn on their dresses. I have no doubt that you will find plenty of other things to titivate with, but Christmas is a-coming and I have a quilt to finish!

Binding

22 Bind the quilt using at least a 2¾in (7cm) wide double binding – see page 101 for instructions. Add a label to the back of the quilt to finish (see page 101).

Christmas Bunting

I just love decorating my house at Christmas and never get wrapped up with all the expensive designer hype. I have a lovely collection of vintage paper decorations which are getting a bit tatty, so I came up with this alternative that should last forever and will not only give my kids great festive memories but all my millions of grandchildren to come! It's easy to make, so get cracking!

Finished size: 77in (195.5cm) long x 7½in (19cm) deep
Techniques: Using templates (page 96) ● Fusible webbing (page 96) ● Appliqué (page 98) ● Ric-rac (page 99) ● Binding (page 101)

Ingredients

- o Two fat quarters of co-ordinating fabric (or lots of scraps)
- o Thin cotton wadding ¼yd (0.25m)
- o Binding 2yd (2m) of 3in (7.6cm) wide (if using check fabric make sure it's cut on the bias)
- o Wide ric-rac braid 6yd (5.5m) and narrow 16in (40.6cm)
- o Fat eighth of fabric for lettering
- o Fat eighth of fusible webbing
- o Cream, green, golden and brown wool/mix felt for decorations each 10in (25.4cm) square
- o Decorative buttons:
  two star buttons for top of tree;
  ten small black buttons for gingerbread man and snowmen eyes;
  ten small heart buttons for gingerbread man and snowmen;
  four small pearly white buttons for mistletoe

Making the flags

1 Enlarge the flag template on page 111 by 200% on a photocopier. Trace the pattern and cut out eight flags from main fabric (different fabrics or all the same – see Quick Tip below). Cut another eight flags from the lining fabric, and then eight from the thin cotton wadding, but make them ½in (1.3cm) bigger all the way around to allow for any discrepancies later on.

2 Enlarge the templates on page 119 by 200% on a photocopier. Using these patterns, blanket stitch appliqué the letters NOEL on four of the flags. On the other four flags appliqué two mistletoe motifs and two Christmas trees. Note: the tree branches are added later in ric-rac but are given in the template to allow you to make them from fabric if you prefer. Don't add any trimmings and finery as these will come later.

3 Cut eight pieces of wide ric-rac 16in (40.6cm) long. Sew the ric-rac to the right side of the main flags. Make sure the edge of the ric-rac lines up with the edge of the bunting (see diagram page 99). *Do not sew along the top edge.* When you come to sew around the bottom of the bunting, gently ease around the curve.

Quick Tip. . .
To make the most economical use of the fat quarter, cut the flags one the right way and the next upside down and so on.

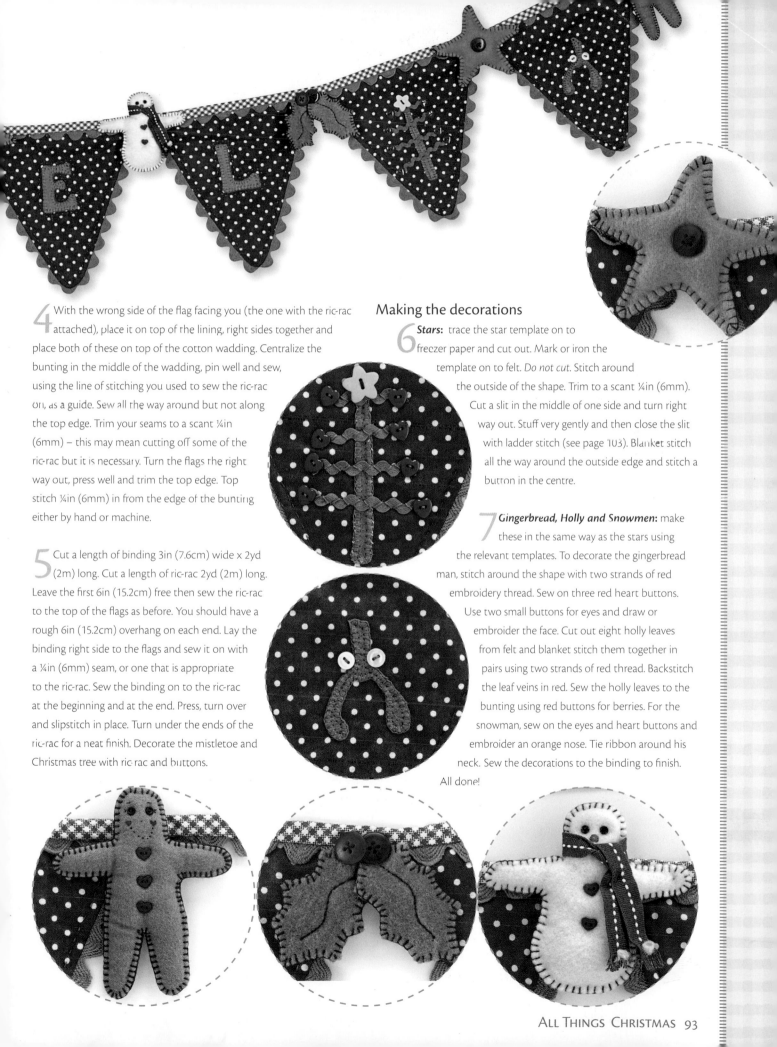

4 With the wrong side of the flag facing you (the one with the ric-rac attached), place it on top of the lining, right sides together and place both of these on top of the cotton wadding. Centralize the bunting in the middle of the wadding, pin well and sew, using the line of stitching you used to sew the ric-rac on, as a guide. Sew all the way around but not along the top edge. Trim your seams to a scant ¼in (6mm) – this may mean cutting off some of the ric-rac but it is necessary. Turn the flags the right way out, press well and trim the top edge. Top stitch ¼in (6mm) in from the edge of the bunting either by hand or machine.

5 Cut a length of binding 3in (7.6cm) wide x 2yd (2m) long. Cut a length of ric-rac 2yd (2m) long. Leave the first 6in (15.2cm) free then sew the ric-rac to the top of the flags as before. You should have a rough 6in (15.2cm) overhang on each end. Lay the binding right side to the flags and sew it on with a ¼in (6mm) seam, or one that is appropriate to the ric-rac. Sew the binding on to the ric-rac at the beginning and at the end. Press, turn over and slipstitch in place. Turn under the ends of the ric-rac for a neat finish. Decorate the mistletoe and Christmas tree with ric-rac and buttons.

Making the decorations

6 **Stars:** trace the star template on to freezer paper and cut out. Mark or iron the template on to felt. *Do not cut.* Stitch around the outside of the shape. Trim to a scant ¼in (6mm). Cut a slit in the middle of one side and turn right way out. Stuff very gently and then close the slit with ladder stitch (see page 103). Blanket stitch all the way around the outside edge and stitch a button in the centre.

7 **Gingerbread, Holly and Snowmen:** make these in the same way as the stars using the relevant templates. To decorate the gingerbread man, stitch around the shape with two strands of red embroidery thread. Sew on three red heart buttons. Use two small buttons for eyes and draw or embroider the face. Cut out eight holly leaves from felt and blanket stitch them together in pairs using two strands of red thread. Backstitch the leaf veins in red. Sew the holly leaves to the bunting using red buttons for berries. For the snowman, sew on the eyes and heart buttons and embroider an orange nose. Tie ribbon around his neck. Sew the decorations to the binding to finish. All done!

Equipment and Materials

Equipment

There are many tools and pieces of equipment you could buy for patchwork and quilting but you can make the projects in this book with the minimum. A basic tool kit is really all you need.

Basic Tool Kit

- Cutting ruler
- Tape measure
- Needles
- Pins
- Safety pins
- Pincushion
- Needle threader
- Scissors
- Stitch ripper
- Propelling pencil
- Pigma pens
- ¼in (6mm) tape
- Masking tape
- Chop stick
- Fusible webbing
- Rotary cutter
- Cutting mat
- Spray starch
- Iron
- Sewing machine

Materials

We all have our favourite materials and embellishments: some of mine are described here and shown in the pictures below and opposite.

Fabrics

I always try to use 100% cotton in all my projects and obviously patchwork fabrics work best because they are all the same weight, but sometimes it is great to use other fabrics, such as denim (a special favourite of mine), which I used in the picnic rug on page 36. In the crazy sofa throw on page 78 I used cotton velvet, silks brocades, needlecords and furnishing fabrics, although they were all still cotton.

Fabrics used to back quilts or to line projects such as bags can really be anything you like. I love to put unusual fabrics on the back of quilts and to line my bags – it's great to open a bag and spy a gorgeous lining. For snugly quilts I use minkee or fleece on the back. My kids really love the cosy effect, and even though these materials are not cotton, they are fine if pinned to the quilt top well. Quilting isn't a problem if you use a really sharp needle.

Wadding (batting)

Quilt wadding is rated by its weight and is sold in standard sizes and by the yard or metre. It is available in polyester, cotton, wool, silk and various blends and for hand and machine quilting. I use a cotton/polyester 80/20 mix and prefer finer wadding that quilts well with chunky quilting stitches. When making a wall hanging, I prefer Warm and Natural wadding, which is a bit thicker and hangs flat. Unconventional but, oh so snugly, is fleece and minkie – my children prefer quilts backed in this super-soft material. Minkie machine quilts like a dream if prepared well. I do not put wadding in the quilt when I am using a fleece back.

Safety Pins and Spray Glue

Before quilting, the three layers of a quilt – front, wadding and backing – need to be temporarily fixed together by some means. I rarely tack the three layers together, preferring to use safety pins. I am, however, quite vigilant about pinning every 3in– 4in (7.6cm–10.2cm), which avoids puckers on the back. My other favourite method is spray adhesive (which must be removed by washing). I like the 505 brand as this doesn't clog the needle. I only use this on small wall hangings and quilts under 24in (60cm) square, as otherwise you have to rope in members of the family to help with the layering! When using spray glues, do protect carpets and flooring and do not be over generous with the spraying. Always read the instructions on the can about health and safety and remember to spray the *wadding* not the quilt top!

Needles

Because I rarely quilt 600 stitches to the inch these days, the quilters 'betweens' needles are of no use to me, so I use a short embroidery crewel needle size 9, which has a nice large eye for threading and is sharp.

Threads

Always buy the best thread you can afford: it doesn't make sense to spend a fortune on fabric and then buy cheap threads. I mostly quilt with coton à broder, which comes in a huge variety of colours and is just delicious to use. I machine quilt with ordinary cotton thread.

Fusible Webbing

Fusible webs are glue- or plastic-based products that are used to bond one fabric to another. They can be single-sided or double-sided. See overleaf for descriptions of some fusible webbings and their use. I couldn't live without this product; it 'glues' one piece of fabric to another using the heat of the iron – perfect for appliqué. You will still have raw edges that need to be attached with a stitch but for my country style this is just perfect.

Freezer Paper

This is a useful product that you can use with templates and appliqué for patchwork. Patchwork and quilting shops sell freezer paper and you can also get it from websites (see page 120). See overleaf for using freezer paper.

Notions and Fasteners

I just love the unusual little fasteners and trims you can buy that give your work a professional finish and make it stand out from the rest. They are not always easy to find so scour your local haberdashery and patchwork shops. If all else fails try a search engine on the Web.

Braids and Trims

Ric-rac is my favourite trim. If your patchwork shop doesn't stock it, and they should, scrapbook suppliers will have it, along with lots of other gorgeous braids. I recommend that you try your local shops first, then the Web: remember 'use it or lose it' – small business are struggling and while parcels might be exciting there is nothing like seeing and fondling the real thing. Of course you can substitute ric-rac for any other braid you may find – don't be put off making a project just because it may not look exactly the same as mine. I encourage you to 'follow your own star'.

Buttons and Charms

As you may have guessed I am just passionate about buttons – you ought to see my collection! Recycled ones are often the most exciting and charming, so rummage through grandma's boxes and then start collecting yourself (see Suppliers) or button boxes will become extinct!

Techniques

This section describes the basic techniques you will need to make and finish off the projects in this book, from using templates to binding a finished quilt. Beginners should find it very useful.

Using Templates

The templates in the end section of the book are all shown at half size, so you need to enlarge them all by 200% on a photocopier to bring the patterns up to full size. The templates can then be cut out from the paper and the outline traced on to the fabric, or the paper can be pinned to the fabric and then cut out or sewn close to the edge of the paper. Pattern pieces have the seam allowances included, usually ¼in (6mm) unless otherwise stated. Templates for useful shapes, such as squares and circles can be easily created from the thin card from cereal packets or from template plastic, available from quilting suppliers.

To make a template of a more unusual shape, such as a chair for the seat cover on page 33, take a sheet of newspaper, put it on the chair and mark around the seat. Remembering to allow for ¼in (6mm) seams all round, cut out this shape and then fold the paper in half to see if it is symmetrical. If not, trim it so it is symmetrical and put it back on the chair to make sure it covers well, adjusting the size if necessary.

Tea Dyeing

Fabrics, threads and cords can all be dyed using tea. Place six tea bags in a large bowl, cover with boiling water and then add the item to be dyed. In the case of the Anja doll on page 65, add the already wet calico and piping cord to the bowl. Stir and leave for a couple of hours or over night. Rinse the items in clean water and allow them to dry. Iron the fabric before use to remove any creases.

Using Fusible Webbings

I use fusible webbing all the time on my appliqué. As long as you sew the edges down you get good results, though some have little hiccups you need to be aware of. Tip of the day – read the manufacturer's instructions well before use!

Bondaweb This is nice and fine and sews through really well but doesn't appear to last very long in storage. I find that the fusible film peels off the paper, which is nigh on impossible to get back on; apparently you can prevent this by storing it in the freezer! To solve this, my tip is only buy enough for each project.

Heatnbond Lite The adhesive film on this product is a little thicker than the previous, stores really well, but fixes with a cool, silk setting on the iron. If you forget this and use a hot iron, this will render the adhesive qualities useless – which can be annoying.

Steam-A-Seam 2 Lite This is a lovely product (see Suppliers for sources). It has the ability to stick your appliqué in place temporarily until you then decide to iron it. Great, because when you walk to the iron with your piece of work the appliqué doesn't all fly off.

Using Sew-in Interfacing

This is such a lovely product for making beautiful simple shapes like hearts, leaves and circles, which have their edges turned, because it avoids fiddly needle turning. I used it in the Welcome Sampler Quilt on page 8, on the sunshine block and on also for the heart on the sewing roll on page 70.

Mark the shape you require on to the interfacing with a pencil. Put the piece of fabric that you want to use right sides to the interfacing, pin and then sew on the marked line. Cut around the outside edge of the sewn line, a neat and scant ¼in (6mm). Cut a slit in the interfacing, turn the right way out, finger press and then ladder stitch your shape on to the backing.

Using Freezer Paper

Freezer paper is a useful product for patchwork. It is perfect for using as a reuseable template as one side of it is silicone and irons beautifully on to fabric and can be peeled off without damaging it.

If you cannot get freezer paper, just cut out the templates, pin them in place on to the fabric, mark around the outside edge with a fine pencil, and sew on this pencil line, then cut a scant ¼in (6mm) seam.

Foundation Piecing

Foundation piecing can be confusing, much like trying to pat your head and rub your tummy at the same time, but once mastered the advantages are great and you will be able to make very complicated blocks and angles with precision and ease.

1 See Fig 1 A–F for the basic sequence. Photocopy the pattern templates twice on to cheap paper (this is easier to sew through than expensive, heavier weights). Some people trace the pattern on to lightweight no-iron interfacing. Cut out one paper foundation pattern roughly ¼in (6mm) from the marked outside line. Using the second paper foundation pattern, cut out all the shapes on the inside line. These will be used as cutting out templates for each pattern piece.

2 Take pattern piece number 1, place it on to the wrong side of a piece of fabric, making sure the right side of the pattern piece is facing you. Pin in place and cut out with a *generous* ½in (1.3cm) seam – *this is very important* – don't be mean with fabric until you are more experienced with foundation piecing. Do this with all the other pattern pieces. Pin this piece of fabric on to the wrong side of the template – there will be no markings on this side so make sure you cover the whole shape. You will not be able to see the shape so you may have to hold it up to the light. Pin in place.

3 Fold and finger crease along the line between pieces 1 and 2. Place pattern piece 2, right sides together on to the piece you placed before on the fold line, then move it forward by ¼in (6mm). Pin along the line between 1 and 2, flip it back to check it will cover shape 2, and if all is well, re-adjust your pins so you can sew over them. Turn the fabric and pattern over and sew on the line between 1 and 2 – this will be on the right side of the paper where the pattern is marked, and may feel wrong, but I promise you it is right! Flip back to check all is still well – all of the pattern including the outside seam allowances must now be covered. Trim the seam you have just sewn to a rough ¼in (6mm) and press. Repeat this process with consecutive pattern pieces.

4 Once the block is sewn trim to the correct size, that is, to the *outside* line of the seam allowance. Do not remove the foundation paper until the blocks are sewn together as this will protect any bias edges and help keep them square. When you join the blocks together, use the seam allowance on the papers. Once the blocks are all joined together you can remove the paper.

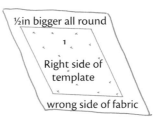

A Cut out the first fabric piece roughly

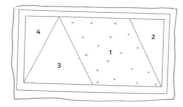

B The foundation pattern cut out roughly

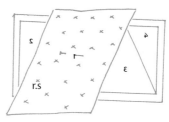

C Fabric piece placed on foundation pattern

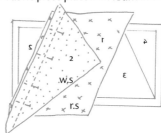

D The second fabric piece pinned right sides to the first piece

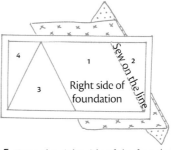

E From the right side of the foundation, sew on the line between 1 and 2

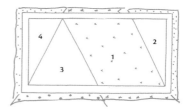

F Trim the finished block to the outside line

Fig 1 The sequence for foundation piecing (A–F)

Crazy Stitch and Flip

This is an easy way to piece together patches for a crazy patchwork look and is used for the seat cover on page 33 and the sewing roll on page 70. You will need a foundation fabric, such as calico and assorted strips or 'chunks' of fabric.

1 I start off with a square that I have cut all the corners off (not in a neat way). I then lay it on the foundation fabric. Lay a strip of fabric along one edge of the patch, right sides together, raw edges matching (see Fig 1A). Sew in place, trim off the extra length of the second fabric and flip it so that it is right side up and press.

2 Now place a different strip or chunk on an adjacent edge of the multi-sided patch. Pin and sew in place as before. Trim the excess, flip the new fabric to the right side and press (1B). Continue to sew all the way around the multi-sided patch in the same manner to cover the middle section of the calico. Vary the angles at which you sew the patches to achieve a non-uniform effect (1C). If there are any gaps that a strip won't cover, cut a square, turn under ¼in (6mm) on three sides (leaving the side hanging off the calico unhemmed) and pin in place. Top sew in place. Once you have covered all the calico, press and then trim the edges of the patchwork even with the calico.

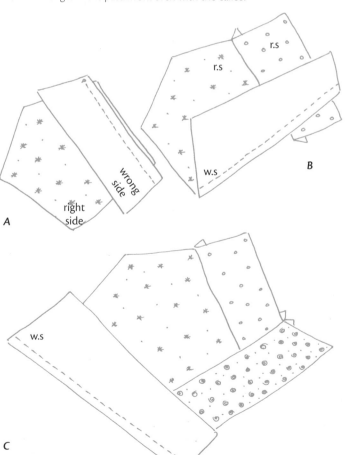

Fig 2 *Stages of the crazy stitch and flip technique (A, B and C)*

Appliqué

Appliqué is the technique of attaching a fabric to a background fabric with hand or machine stitching. Here are a few tips on achieving good results with appliqué. Remember, practise makes perfect. It's far better to make a quilt, finish it, and learn from it than have no quilts at all!

o Always start by giving your sewing machine a little spring clean and a new needle. I like to use the denim variety size 12 or 14 as these are sharp for piecing.

o Reduce your top tension slightly (remember, 'lefty loosey, righty tighty' – silly rhyme but it works a treat). When you are appliquéing by machine you need the top threads to show underneath the work slightly so that you get a nice curved stitch on the top. Practise on identical fabric and layers first.

o Use bobbin fill or ordinary thread in the bobbin, and if you have that special little hole in the arm of your bobbin case, thread your cotton through this to give a better tension.

o Use your needle-down facility if you have one to stop the stitch slipping. Using the knee lift on your machine will help too.

o Always use the correct foot for the job: you need an open-toed embroidery/appliqué foot that has a cut-away on the underside and makes a huge difference by allowing the raised stitch of the appliqué to go under the foot more freely.

o If you have not attached your shapes with fusible webbing (which I recommend), use some thin paper or 'stitch and tear' behind your work when you sew as it prevents ruffled stitching and makes a huge difference.

o Always start by pulling thread up to the top, sew a couple of stitches on top of each other and then cut the thread. This prevents the threads tangling underneath.

o Always cover the edge of the appliqué with a stitch to seal the edges.

o On curves, stop on the outside edge, needle down, foot up, and then turn the fabric. It is better to stop and start a dozen times than try and get round the corner in one foul swoop.

o I now always use the blanket stitch that comes on most new machines and, surprisingly enough, some older ones. With a bit of practise, you can get a great hand look. You can blanket stitch with a thicker thread by putting a larger needle in your machine. The bobbin thread remains unchanged.

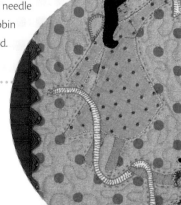

Adding Borders

A border frames the finished quilt nicely and gives you the opportunity to use more lovely fabric! The quilts in this book use butted corners.

1 To find out what length the border should be, measure the width of the quilt through the centre and cut the top and bottom borders to this measurement. Measuring through the centre is more accurate than at the ends, which may have 'spread' a bit during the making of the quilt. Sew the top and bottom borders on using ¼in (6mm) seams and then press (see Fig 3).

2 Now measure the quilt height, again through the centre, including the top and bottom borders you have just added, and cut the side borders to this measurement. Sew the side borders on using ¼in (6mm) seams and then press the seams.

Using Rac-rac Braid

As you might have guessed by now I love this stuff and use it all the time to embellish and highlight my work. I use it to emphasize a row or border (see Fig 4 and the pictures below) and also along the edge of a quilt, sewing it in with the binding (see Fig 5). One of the best things about ric-rac is that if you gather a length along the middle, pull the gathers up, wind the braid into a circle and secure you get a lovely flower!

Ric-rac can be difficult to join but I've found that the best way is to match the 'humps' in the braid by folding one end back and tucking it under the other. I have a favourite stitch for applying ric-rac, which actually quilts as you sew (see Fig 4). I hardly ever sew it on with the machine: I don't like the line down the middle and the machine foot seems to slip off occasionally.

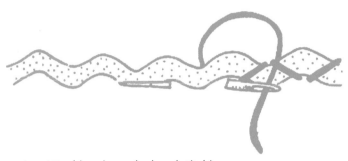

Fig 4 *Attaching ric-rac by hand stitching*

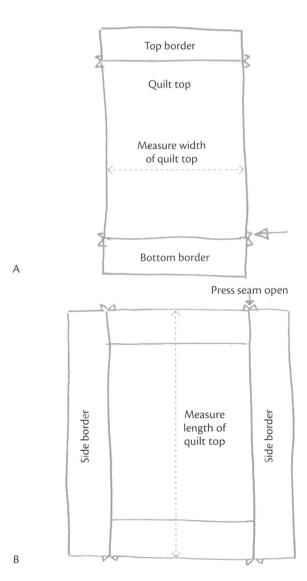

A

Top border

Quilt top

Measure width
of quilt top

Bottom border

Press seam open

Side border

Measure
length of
quilt top

Side border

B

Fig 3 *Adding borders to the top and bottom of the quilt (A) and then to the sides (B)*

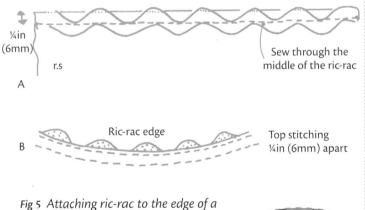

¼in
(6mm)

r.s

A

Sew through the
middle of the ric-rac

Ric-rac edge

B

Top stitching
¼in (6mm) apart

Fig 5 *Attaching ric-rac to the edge of a quilt (A) and then topstitching (B)*

Layering a Quilt

This will be one of the most important things you can do for a quilt. Layer it correctly and it will hang well, have no puckers and look very professional.

1 Before you start, prepare all the fabrics. Cut out your wadding and backing at least 2in (5cm) larger than the quilt top. Press your backing fabric and hang out your wadding or pop it in the tumble dryer to remove creases (do check the wadding manufacturer's instructions first though).

2 Prepare the quilt top by cutting off or tying in any stray ends (guess which method I prefer?), and give the quilt a general iron, sorting out your seam allowances.

3 I use my dining room table or the floor if I need more space – it depends on how good your knees are! Using masking tape, stick the quilt back, wrong side facing you, quite taut to the surface. If you have carpets, use pins with large visible knobs on the ends – for obvious reasons. Place the wadding on top of the quilt back and smooth it out flat (there's no need to secure it). Place the quilt top on centrally. Pin with safety pins every 3in (7.6cm) or so, pinning where you know you will not be sewing. You need to pin this close for good results, so it's no good moaning about running out of pins. Do not forget to pin in the borders of the quilt. If you are pinning on the carpet and find you are attaching your quilt to it, put your cutting mat under the quilt and shuffle it around so you pin on to the mat. We don't want a shag pile where there wasn't one! The final job is to tack the outside edges, ½in (1.3cm) in from the edge of the quilt using huge long stitches. Your work is now ready for quilting.

Quilting

I nearly always use a combination of hand and machine quilting on my quilts. Once the quilt is nicely layered up I 'stabilize' it by machine sewing around all the blocks in the ditch (in the seams) and along all the long borders with a matching thread or an invisible one. I use YLI invisible thread, which is available in smoke and clear, and a large reel lasts for ages. Other types can snag on the reel and be a disaster to use.

Once the quilt is stabilized I can then get to work with my lovely chunky stitching. I can do a nice fine quilting stitch but I just love the effect of the chunky stitch and now do it all the time. I use it for outlining shapes and sewing a freehand wavy line in the borders. No little quilting needles are needed here – a crewel embroidery needle size 9 will do just nicely. A small disadvantage of chunky stitching is that the knot is not always easy to hide in the wadding, so I put the needle in about 1in (2.5cm) away from where I need it, come out at the quilting spot and then do a backstitch to secure.

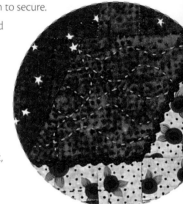

Once I have finished quilting I add the buttons and sew on the ric-rac with the stitch described on page 99. My favourite thread to use is DMC cotton à broder. It is single stranded, which is why I like it, and is available in a huge range of colours. If your local needlecraft store doesn't stock it, they can order it.

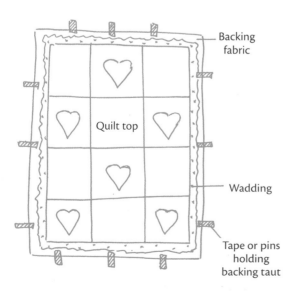

Backing fabric

Quilt top

Wadding

Tape or pins holding backing taut

Fig 6 *Layering a quilt*

Quick Tip...
To prepare a skein of thread for easy use, open out the skein and cut just pass the knot, so you have one long length. Fold it in half, put the fold over a door knob, divide the thread into three and plait it. Secure the end with an elastic band if you wish. When you need a thread just pull one out from the folded end – clever, and no tangling.

Binding

Binding your quilt is the last stage. For my bindings I cut 2¾in (7cm) wide strips across the width of the fabric. I join these together and then fold the total length of binding in half lengthways and press.

1 To begin the binding of the quilt follow Fig 7, laying the binding along one side of the quilt, matching the raw edges (A). Start 6in (15.2cm) in from the beginning of your binding and sew using a chubby ¼in (6mm) seam. Stitch until you reach one corner and stop the same distance from the end as your seam allowance.

2 Pull the work away from the machine and fold the binding up and away from you towards the north, so that it is aligned with the edge of the quilt (B). It must be straight.

3 Holding the corner, fold the binding back down south, aligning it with the raw edge and the folded corner square (C). Pin and sew over the fold, continuing down the next edge. Repeat with the other corners.

4 When you reach your starting point stop 6in (15.2cm) from the start. Fold back the beginning and the end of the binding, so that they touch each other, mark these folds with a pin and cut the binding ¼in (6mm) from the pin. Open out the binding and join with a ¼in (6mm) seam. Press the seam open, refold and then slipstitch in place. When you fold over the binding to slipstitch or top stitch it in place, the mitres will miraculously fall in place and can be slipstitched closed (D). Fig 7E shows how to join the two ends of the binding.

Labelling Your Quilt

This is so very important. I collect old quilts and none of them (except one) have any date, place or name of the maker. It would be so lovely for me to have a name to connect the quilt with and know the reason why it was made and who it was for. I have one lovely old English quilt dated and named E Rees 10.1858, and with the help of an enthusiatic amateur genealogist, and from knowing it was from the local area, we found Emily Rees, a piano teacher who had once lived not far from my home.

So let's not make it so difficult for future generations: sign and date your quilt, tell the story of why you made it and who it was for. In most patchwork shops you can buy permanent ink pens that write beautifully on fabric. Make a label by fraying the edge of a square of calico, write your information on it and stitch it on the back of a quilt with a running stitch. You can also buy labels just for this job. If you are badly bitten by the quilting bug, you could piece a little block with a calico centre and use that as a label.

I also love adding the odd little designer tab here and there on my work, as they make projects look really professional. Just cut an inch of cute ribbon or tape, fold it in half and add it in a seam. I've used tabs on the little bears, Clarence, the stripy bag, sewing roll and the slippers.

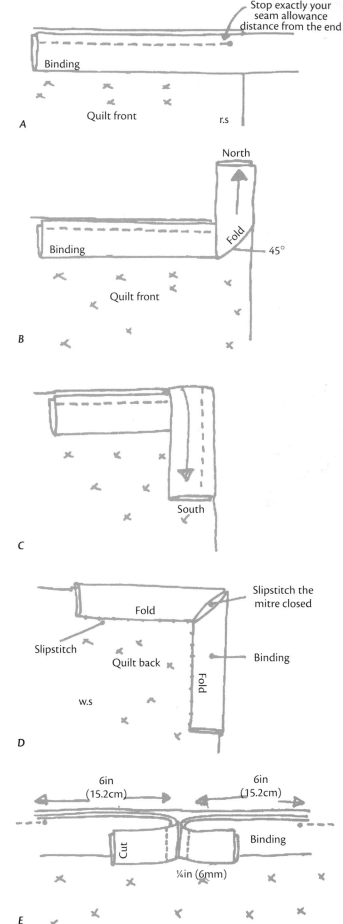

Fig 7A–E Stages to be followed when binding a quilt

Stitches

Various stitches are used in the projects in the book: some are functional, for example to sew up openings or gaps in seams; others are decorative, used to embellish patchwork projects. To work the stitches, follow these simple diagrams.

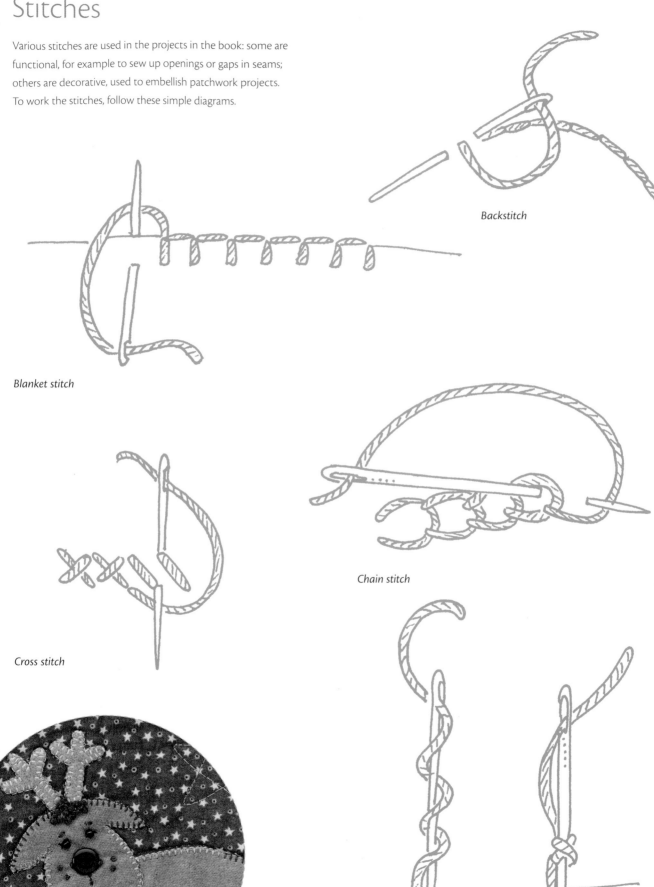

Backstitch

Blanket stitch

Chain stitch

Cross stitch

French knot

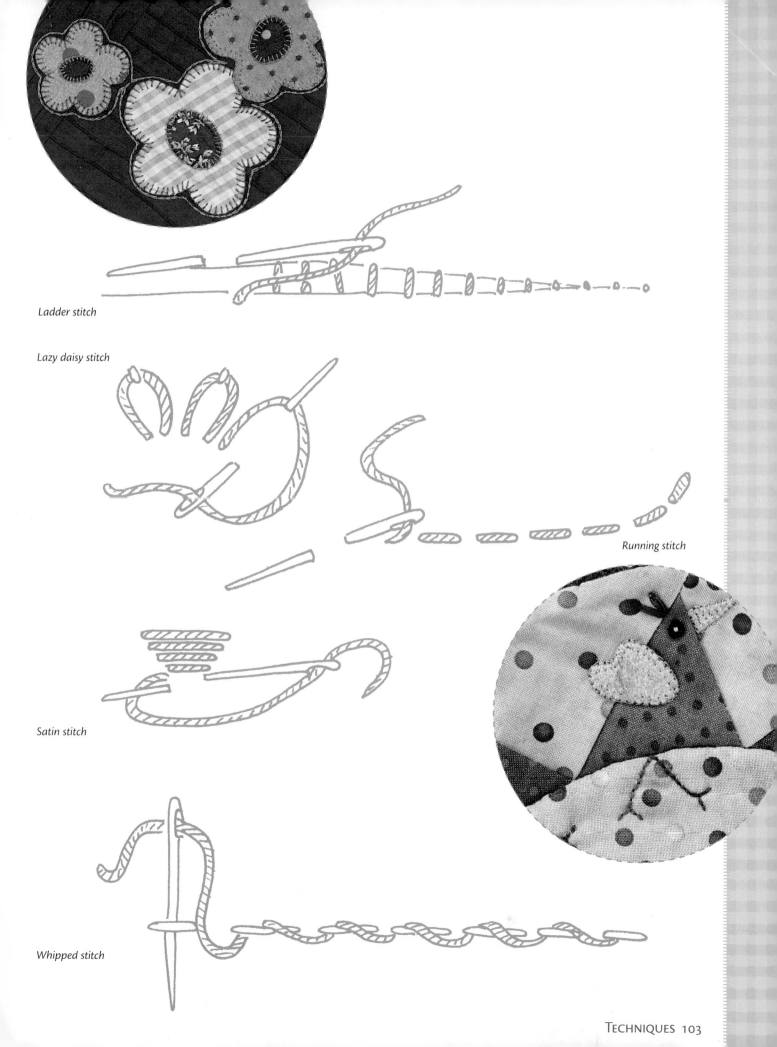

Ladder stitch

Lazy daisy stitch

Running stitch

Satin stitch

Whipped stitch

Templates

The templates given on the following pages have all been reduced by 50% to fit as many projects as possible into the book. You will therefore need to *enlarge all the patterns by 200% on a photocopier* – which you may do as long as the templates are for your own private use. All patterns are drawn in reverse so that they will be the right way round when you come to fuse and sew them. See page 96 for advice on using templates.

Tree templates for foundation piecing
Enlarge by 200%
Make 1 of each

Tree A   Tree B

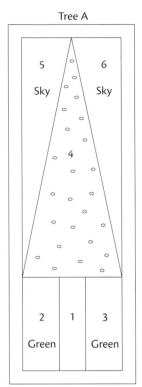

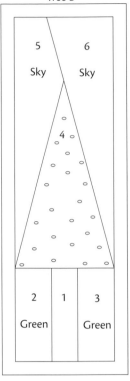

× Button

Heart template
Enlarge by 200%
Make 4

Circular window template
Enlarge by 200%
Make 1

WELCOME QUILT
(page 8)
Enlarge all by 200%

Sunshine template
Enlarge by 200%
Make 1

← Stitch along this curved edge

Birdhouse templates
Enlarge by 200%
Make 1 of each

Flying Geese template for foundation piecing
Enlarge by 200%
Make 2

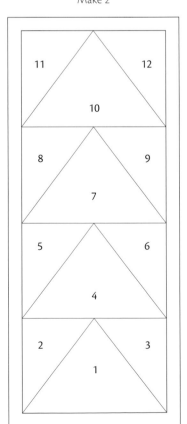

House roof template for foundation piecing
Enlarge by 200%
Make 1

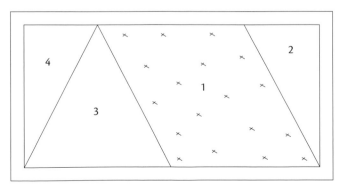

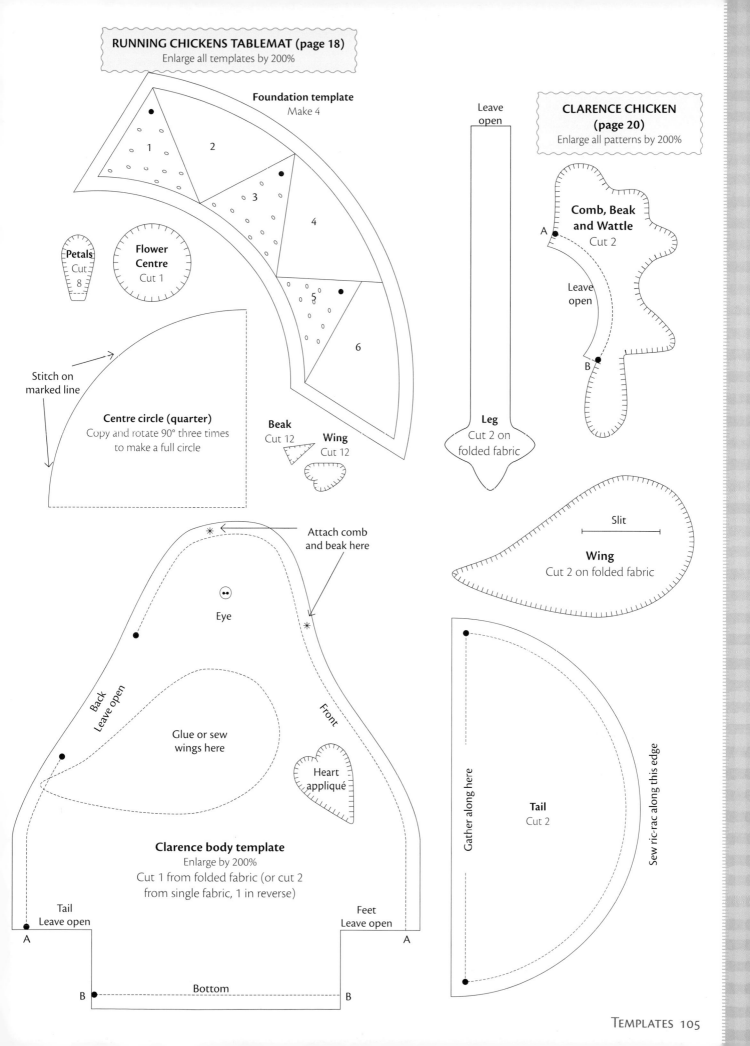

RUNNING CHICKENS TABLEMAT (page 18)
Enlarge all templates by 200%

Foundation template
Make 4

1
2
3
4
5
6

Petals
Cut 8

Flower Centre
Cut 1

Stitch on marked line

Centre circle (quarter)
Copy and rotate 90° three times
to make a full circle

Beak
Cut 12

Wing
Cut 12

Leave open

CLARENCE CHICKEN (page 20)
Enlarge all patterns by 200%

Comb, Beak and Wattle
Cut 2

A

Leave open

B

Leg
Cut 2 on folded fabric

Slit

Wing
Cut 2 on folded fabric

Attach comb and beak here

Eye

Back
Leave open

Front

Glue or sew wings here

Heart appliqué

Clarence body template
Enlarge by 200%
Cut 1 from folded fabric (or cut 2
from single fabric, 1 in reverse)

Tail
Leave open

Feet
Leave open

A

A

B

Bottom

B

Gather along here

Tail
Cut 2

Sew ric-rac along this edge

ROCK-A-BYE BABY QUILT
(page 24)
Enlarge all by 200%

Big bear body
Cut 1 in gingham

Baby bear
position

Cut here

Cut here

Bear templates
Enlarge all by 200%

Legs
Cut 1 in gingham

Baby bear
Cut 1

Place ear
here

**Baby bear
leg**
Cut 1

**Baby bear
ear**
Cut 1
in minkie

Baby bear arm
Cut 1

Head
Cut 1

Big bear inner ears
Cut 1 of each in linen

Big bear muzzle
Cut 1 in linen

Heart templates
Enlarge by 200%

abc def ghi
jkl mno pqr
stu v wx y3

Large alphabet templates
Enlarge by 200%

ROCK-A-BYE BABY QUILT
Small alphabet and numbers templates
Enlarge by 200%

abcdefghij

klmnopqrst

uvwxyз

0123456789

TED BEAR (page 27)
Bear templates
Enlarge all templates by 200%

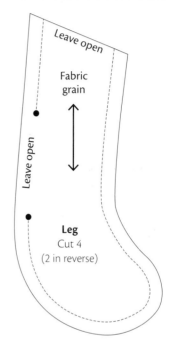

Leave open

Fabric grain

Leave open

Leg
Cut 4
(2 in reverse)

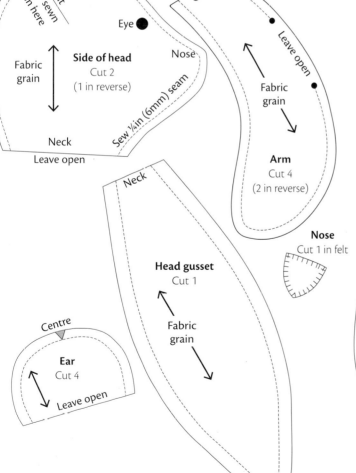

A

Cut

Ear sewn in here

Eye

Nose

Side of head
Cut 2
(1 in reverse)

Fabric grain

Sew ¼in (6mm) seam

Neck

Leave open

Open

Leave open

Fabric grain

Arm
Cut 4
(2 in reverse)

Neck

Head gusset
Cut 1

Fabric grain

Nose

Centre

Ear
Cut 4

Leave open

Nose
Cut 1 in felt

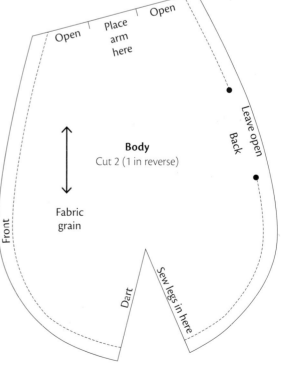

Open | Place arm here | Open

Leave open

Back

Body
Cut 2 (1 in reverse)

Fabric grain

Front

Dart

Sew legs in here

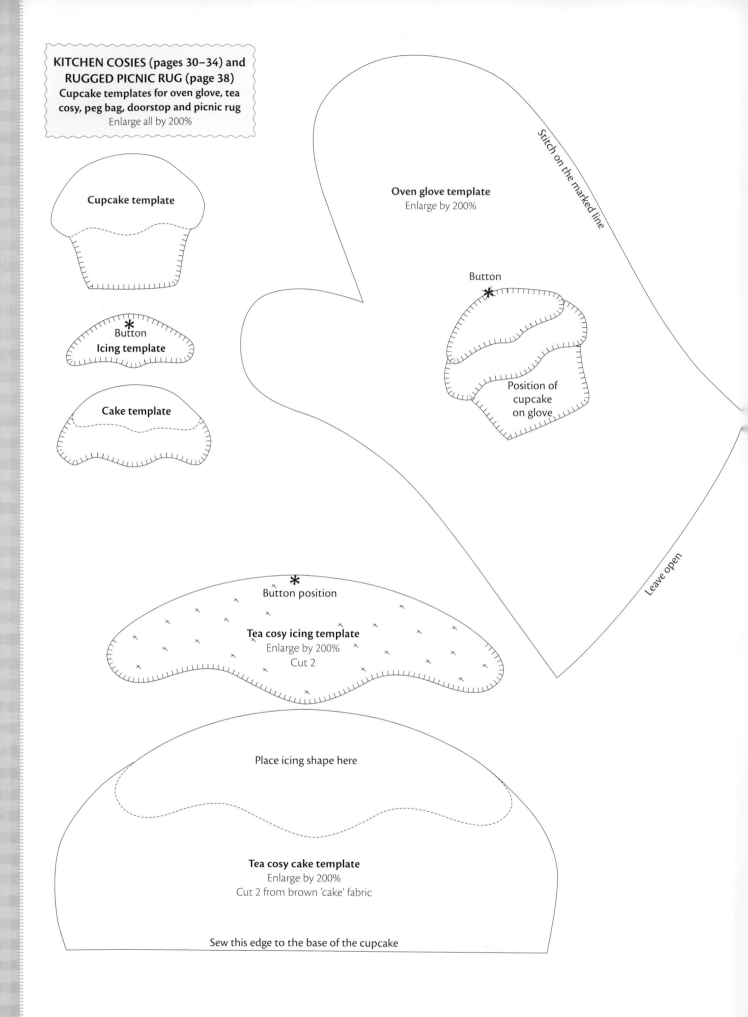

KITCHEN COSIES (pages 30–34) and RUGGED PICNIC RUG (page 38)
Cupcake templates for oven glove, tea cosy, peg bag, doorstop and picnic rug
Enlarge all by 200%

Cupcake template

Button
Icing template

Cake template

Oven glove template
Enlarge by 200%

Stitch on the marked line

Button

Position of cupcake on glove

Leave open

*
Button position

Tea cosy icing template
Enlarge by 200%
Cut 2

Place icing shape here

Tea cosy cake template
Enlarge by 200%
Cut 2 from brown 'cake' fabric

Sew this edge to the base of the cupcake

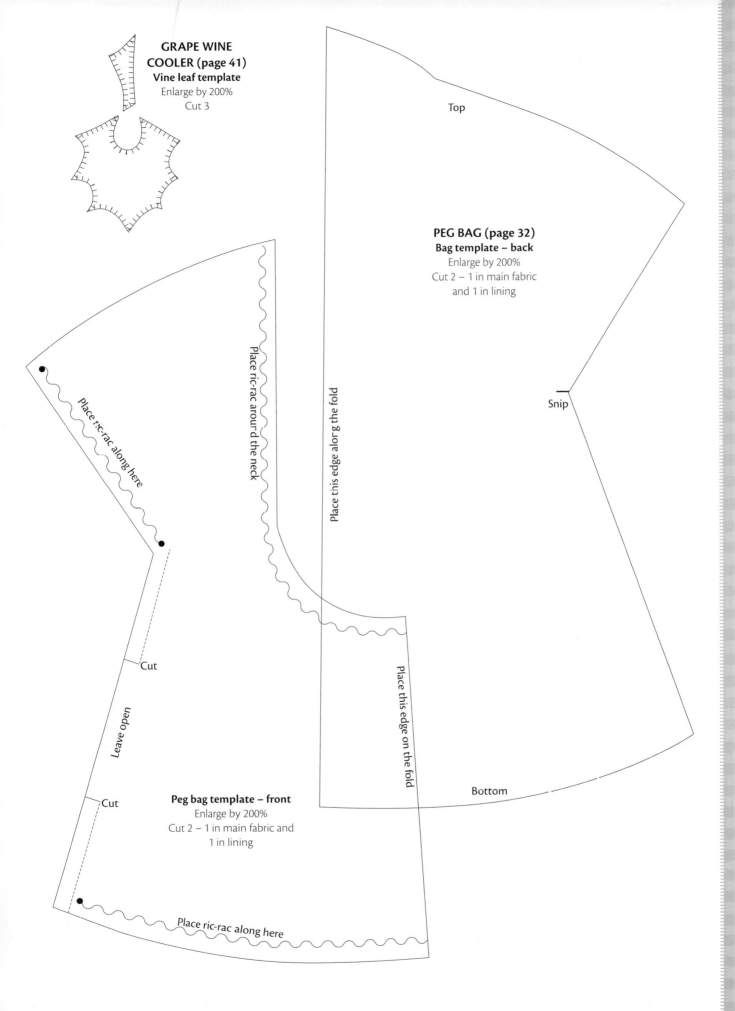

**GRAPE WINE
COOLER (page 41)**
Vine leaf template
Enlarge by 200%
Cut 3

Top

PEG BAG (page 32)
Bag template – back
Enlarge by 200%
Cut 2 – 1 in main fabric
and 1 in lining

Snip

Place ric-rac along here

Place ric-rac around the neck

Place this edge along the fold

Place this edge on the fold

Cut

Leave open

Cut

Peg bag template – front
Enlarge by 200%
Cut 2 – 1 in main fabric and
1 in lining

Bottom

Place ric-rac along here

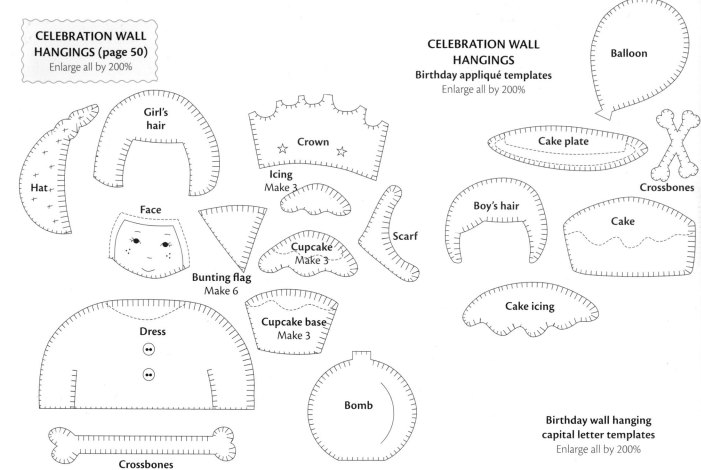

CELEBRATION WALL HANGINGS (page 50)
Enlarge all by 200%

Girl's hair

Hat

Face

Crown

Icing
Make 3

Scarf

Cupcake
Make 3

Bunting flag
Make 6

Cupcake base
Make 3

Dress

Bomb

Crossbones
Make 2

CELEBRATION WALL HANGINGS
Birthday appliqué templates
Enlarge all by 200%

Balloon

Cake plate

Crossbones

Boy's hair

Cake

Cake icing

Birthday wall hanging capital letter templates
Enlarge all by 200%

a b c d e f g h i
j k l m n o p q r
s t u v w x y 3

A B C D E F G H I J
K L M N O P Q R
S T U V W X Y Z

1 2 3 4 5 6 7 8 9 0

th st rd nd

Backstitch letter templates
Enlarge all by 200%

A B C D E
F G H I J K
L M N O P
Q R S T
U V W X
Y Z

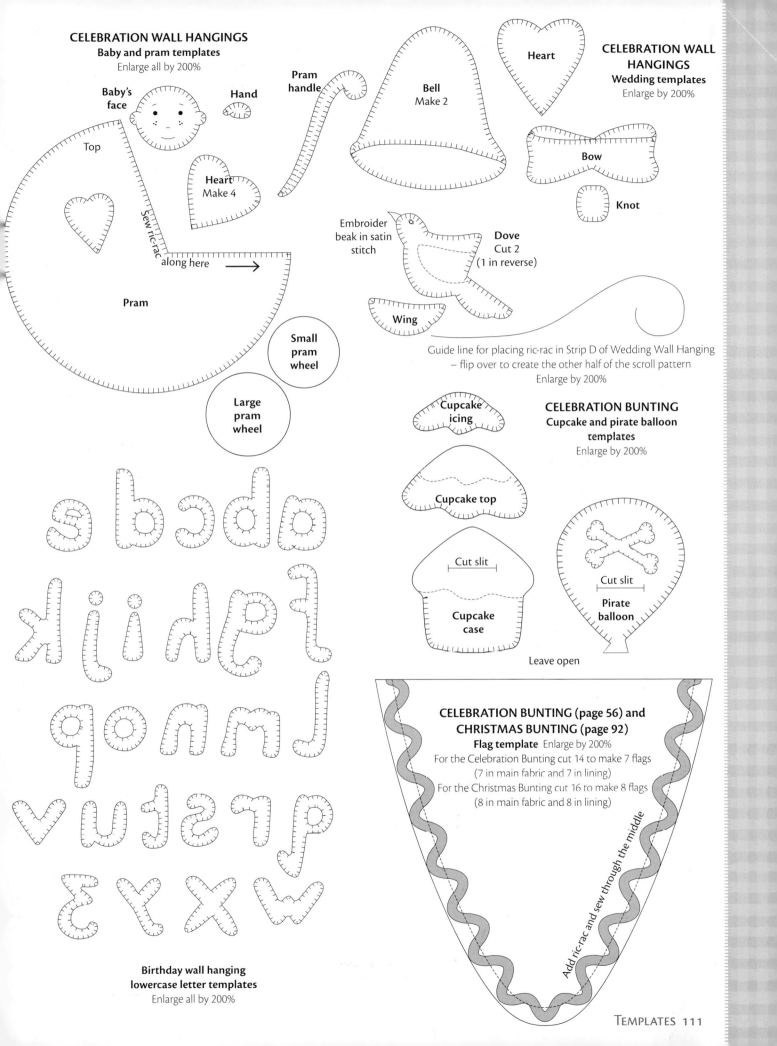

CELEBRATION WALL HANGINGS
Baby and pram templates
Enlarge all by 200%

Baby's face

Hand

Top

Heart
Make 4

Sew ric-rac

along here

Pram

Pram handle

Bell
Make 2

Heart

CELEBRATION WALL HANGINGS
Wedding templates
Enlarge by 200%

Bow

Knot

Embroider beak in satin stitch

Dove
Cut 2
(1 in reverse)

Wing

Guide line for placing ric-rac in Strip D of Wedding Wall Hanging – flip over to create the other half of the scroll pattern
Enlarge by 200%

Small pram wheel

Large pram wheel

Cupcake icing

CELEBRATION BUNTING
Cupcake and pirate balloon templates
Enlarge by 200%

Cupcake top

Cut slit

Cupcake case

Pirate balloon

Cut slit

Leave open

CELEBRATION BUNTING (page 56) and CHRISTMAS BUNTING (page 92)
Flag template Enlarge by 200%
For the Celebration Bunting cut 14 to make 7 flags
(7 in main fabric and 7 in lining)
For the Christmas Bunting cut 16 to make 8 flags
(8 in main fabric and 8 in lining)

Add ric-rac and sew through the middle

Birthday wall hanging lowercase letter templates
Enlarge all by 200%

Angel 1 templates
Enlarge by 200%

Jacket

Hair

Dress

Hands

Wings

Face

Feet

Flower templates
Enlarge by 200%

Small flower for central panel

Angel 2 templates
Enlarge by 200%

Hair

Feet

Face

Arm

Dress

Arm

Pinafore

DANCING ANGELS QUILT
(page 60)
Enlarge by 200%

Angel 4 templates
Enlarge by 200%

Angel 5 templates
Enlarge by 200%

Face

Hair

Hands

Wing

Feet

Dress

Neck

Hair

Dress

Petticoat edge

Hands

Wings

Feet

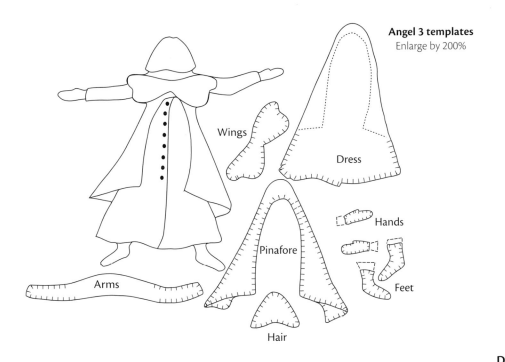

Angel 3 templates
Enlarge by 200%

Wings

Dress

Hands

Pinafore

Feet

Arms

Hair

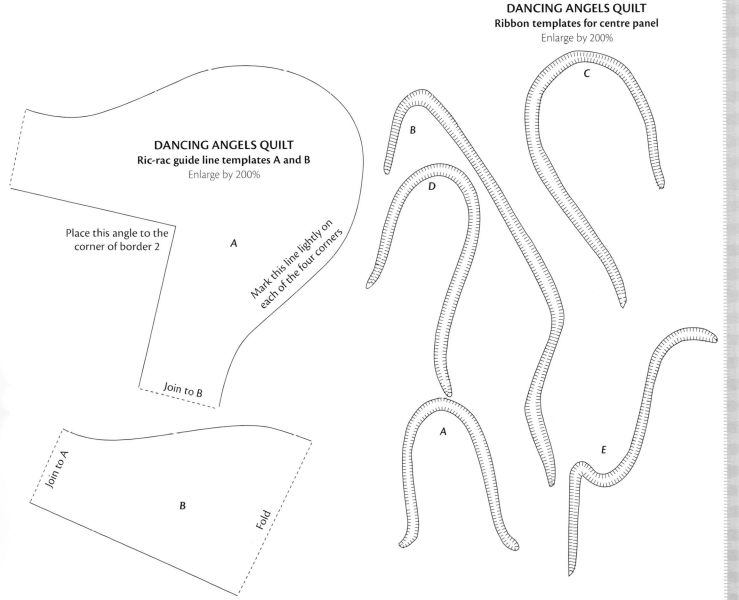

DANCING ANGELS QUILT
Ribbon templates for centre panel
Enlarge by 200%

C

B

D

DANCING ANGELS QUILT
Ric-rac guide line templates A and B
Enlarge by 200%

Place this angle to the corner of border 2

A

Mark this line lightly on each of the four corners

Join to B

A

Join to A

B

Fold

E

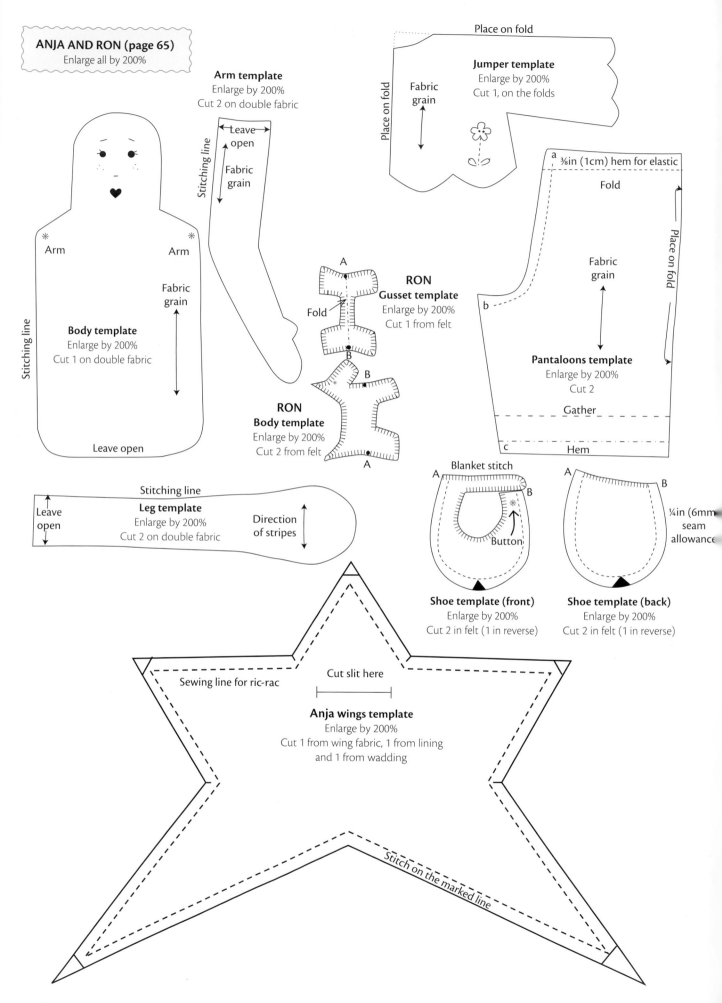

ANJA AND RON (page 65)
Enlarge all by 200%

Arm template
Enlarge by 200%
Cut 2 on double fabric

Stitching line

←Leave open→

Fabric grain

Place on fold

Jumper template
Enlarge by 200%
Cut 1, on the folds

Place on fold

Fabric grain

⅜in (1cm) hem for elastic

a

Fold

Arm

Arm

Fabric grain

Place on fold

Stitching line

Body template
Enlarge by 200%
Cut 1 on double fabric

A

Fold

RON
Gusset template
Enlarge by 200%
Cut 1 from felt

Fabric grain

b

B

B

RON
Body template
Enlarge by 200%
Cut 2 from felt

A

Pantaloons template
Enlarge by 200%
Cut 2

Leave open

Gather

c

Hem

Stitching line

Leg template
Enlarge by 200%
Cut 2 on double fabric

Leave open

Direction of stripes

Blanket stitch

A

B

A

B

¼in (6mm) seam allowance

Button

Shoe template (front)
Enlarge by 200%
Cut 2 in felt (1 in reverse)

Shoe template (back)
Enlarge by 200%
Cut 2 in felt (1 in reverse)

Cut slit here

Sewing line for ric-rac

Anja wings template
Enlarge by 200%
Cut 1 from wing fabric, 1 from lining
and 1 from wadding

Stitch on the marked line

COSY CRAZY THROW
(page 78)
Enlarge by 200%

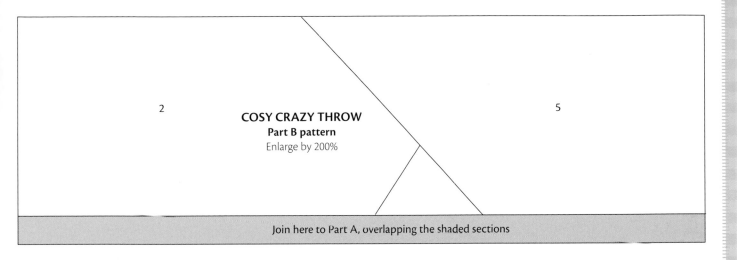

2

5

COSY CRAZY THROW
Part B pattern
Enlarge by 200%

Join here to Part A, overlapping the shaded sections

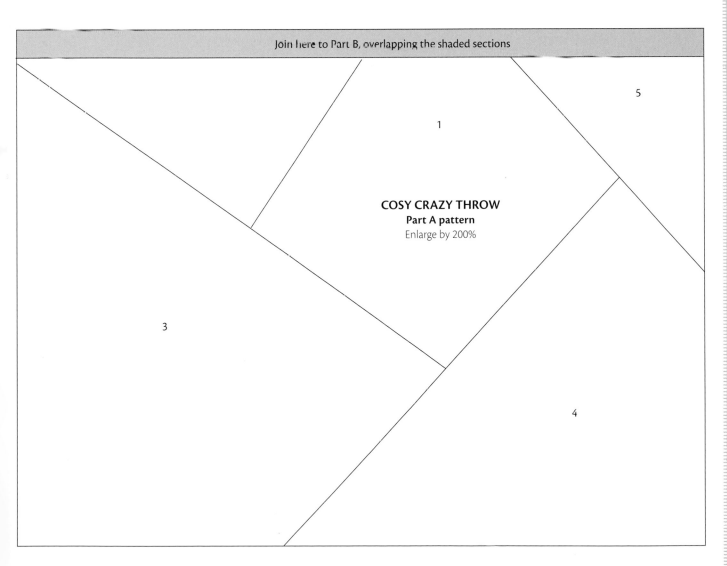

Join here to Part B, overlapping the shaded sections

1

5

COSY CRAZY THROW
Part A pattern
Enlarge by 200%

3

4

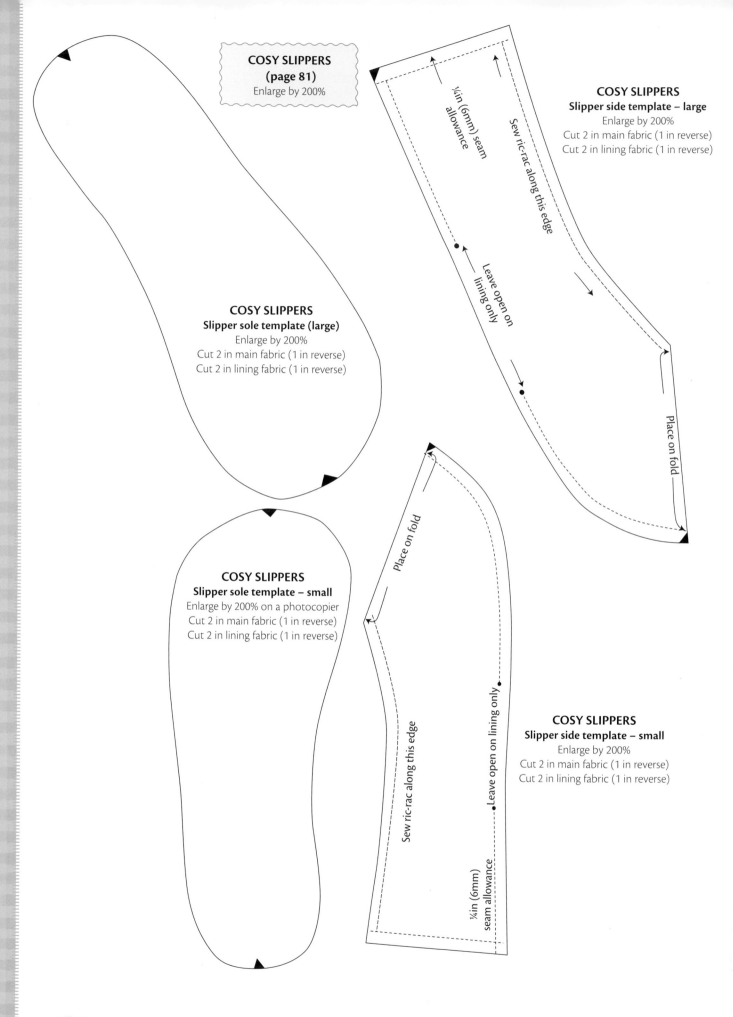

COSY SLIPPERS
(page 81)
Enlarge by 200%

COSY SLIPPERS
Slipper sole template (large)
Enlarge by 200%
Cut 2 in main fabric (1 in reverse)
Cut 2 in lining fabric (1 in reverse)

COSY SLIPPERS
Slipper side template – large
Enlarge by 200%
Cut 2 in main fabric (1 in reverse)
Cut 2 in lining fabric (1 in reverse)

¼in (6mm) seam allowance

Sew ric-rac along this edge

Leave open on lining only

Place on fold

COSY SLIPPERS
Slipper sole template – small
Enlarge by 200% on a photocopier
Cut 2 in main fabric (1 in reverse)
Cut 2 in lining fabric (1 in reverse)

Place on fold

Sew ric-rac along this edge

Leave open on lining only

¼in (6mm) seam allowance

COSY SLIPPERS
Slipper side template – small
Enlarge by 200%
Cut 2 in main fabric (1 in reverse)
Cut 2 in lining fabric (1 in reverse)

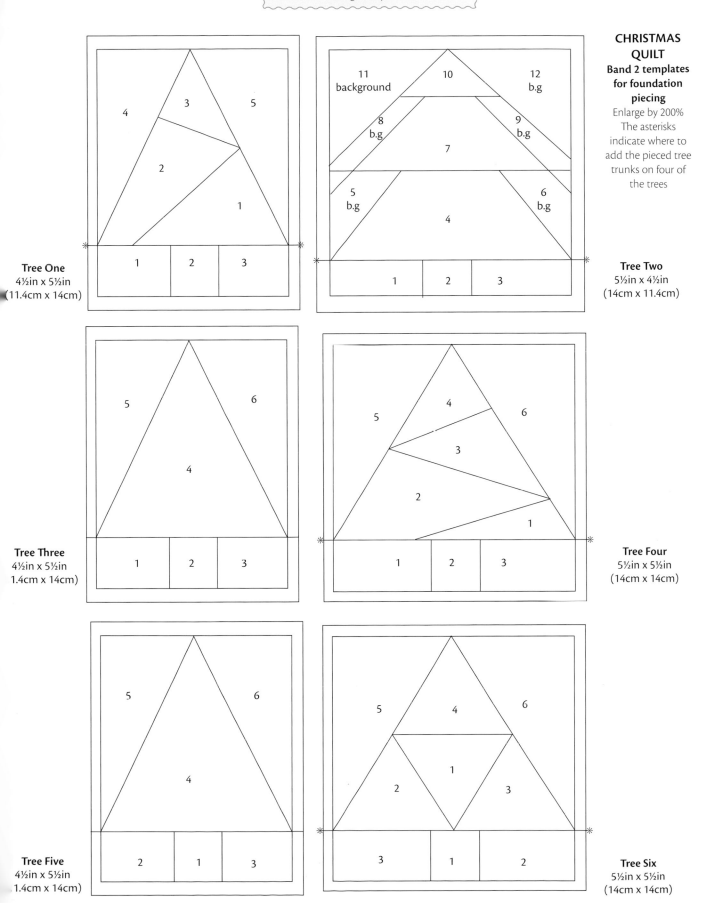

CHRISTMAS
QUILT
**Band 2 templates
for foundation
piecing**
Enlarge by 200%
The asterisks
indicate where to
add the pieced tree
trunks on four of
the trees

Tree One
4½in x 5½in
(11.4cm x 14cm)

Tree Two
5½in x 4½in
(14cm x 11.4cm)

Tree Three
4½in x 5½in
1.4cm x 14cm)

Tree Four
5½in x 5½in
(14cm x 14cm)

Tree Five
4½in x 5½in
1.4cm x 14cm)

Tree Six
5½in x 5½in
(14cm x 14cm)

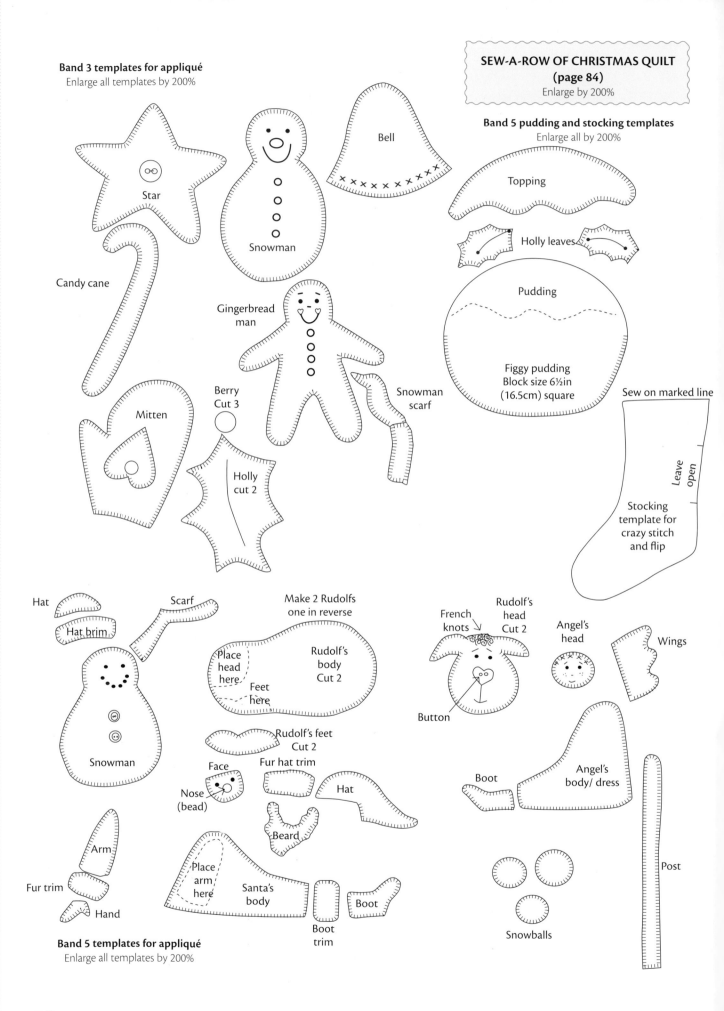

Band 3 templates for appliqué
Enlarge all templates by 200%

Band 5 pudding and stocking templates
Enlarge all by 200%

Star

Bell

Topping

Candy cane

Snowman

Holly leaves

Gingerbread
man

Pudding

Berry
Cut 3

Snowman
scarf

Figgy pudding
Block size 6½in
(16.5cm) square

Mitten

Sew on marked line

Holly
cut 2

Leave open

Stocking
template for
crazy stitch
and flip

Hat

Scarf

Make 2 Rudolfs
one in reverse

French
knots

Rudolf's
head
Cut 2

Angel's
head

Wings

Hat brim

Place
head
here

Rudolf's
body
Cut 2

Feet
here

Button

Snowman

Rudolf's feet
Cut 2

Boot

Angel's
body/ dress

Face

Fur hat trim

Nose
(bead)

Hat

Post

Arm

Beard

Fur trim

Place
arm
here

Santa's
body

Boot

Hand

Boot
trim

Snowballs

Band 5 templates for appliqué
Enlarge all templates by 200%

CHRISTMAS QUILT
Border templates for appliqué
Enlarge all templates by 200%

Top
Star

Border angel 1

Hair

Wings

Face

Hand

Tree

Hand

Dress

Feet

Face
Hair

Border angel 2

Arm
Cut 2

Wings

Feet

Hand

Dress

Hand

Hand
Cut 2

Sleigh top

Runner

Sack

Sleigh

CHRISTMAS BUNTING
Appliqué templates
Enlarge all templates by 200%

Mistletoe
Make 2

Buttons

Tree
Make 2

Ric-rac

Slit

Slit

Holly leaves
Cut 8 to make 4

Stars
Cut 4 to make 2

Snip
Snip
Snip
Snip
Snip
Snip

Leave open

Snip

Snip
Snip

Snip

Leave open

Snowman
Cut 4 to make 2

Gingerbread man
Cut 4 to make 2

CHRISTMAS QUILT (page 84) and
CHRISTMAS BUNTING (page 92)
Noel letters templates
Enlarge all templates by 200%

NOEL

Suppliers

UK

The Button Company
Tel: 01243 775462
www.buttoncompany.co.uk
*For an amazing array of buttons
and charms for crafts*

Daisy Chain Designs
Meadowsweet, Caldicotts
Lane, Lower Dicker, East
Sussex BN27 4BG
Tel: 01323 848894
www.daisychaindesigns.co.uk
*Suppliers of quilting and patchwork
patterns, kits, fabrics, buttons,
ric-racs and ribbons*

Dandelion Designs
37 Summerheath Road, Hailsham,
East Sussex BN273DS
www.dandeliondesigns.co.uk
*Supplier of Mandy Shaw's
patchwork and quilting patterns,
ric-rac braid, tapes, bag fasteners,
fusible webbing, freezer paper,
cotton à broder, buttons and
general haberdashery*

The Patchwork Dog and Basket
The Needlemakers, West Street,
Lewes, East Sussex BN7 2NZ
Tel: 01273 483886
www.patchworkdogandbasket.co.uk
*A delightful shop in an old needle-
making factory, with cafés and
other shops selling treats for the
patchworker including fabrics,
buttons and old quilts*

Puddleducks
116 St John's Hill, Sevenoaks,
Kent TN13 3PD
Tel: 01732 743642
Email: enquiries@
puddleducksquilts.co.uk
www.quiltshopuk.co.uk
*Patchwork and quilting shop selling
lovely fabrics*

Pumpkin Patch
10a St Mary's Walk, Hailsham, East
Sussex BN27 1AF
Tel: 01323 442821
*Patchwork and quilting shop selling
lovely fabrics*

US

The City Quilter
157 West 24th Street, New York,
NY 1011
Tel: 212 807 0390
*For patchwork and quilting supplies
(shop and mail order)*

Connecting Threads
13118 NE 4th Street, Vancouver,
WA 98684
Tel: 1 800 574 6454
Email: customerservice@
connectingthreads.com
www.connectingthreads.com
*For general needlework and
patchwork and quilting supplies*

eQuilter.com
5455 Spine Road, Suite E; Boulder,
CO 80301
Tel: USA Toll Free: 877-FABRIC-3
or: 303-527-0856
Email: service@equilter.com
www.eQuilter.com
For patchwork fabrics

Joann Stores, Inc
5555 Darrow Road, Hudson Ohio
Tel: 1 888 739 4120
Email: guest service@jo-annstores.
com
www.joann.com
*For general needlework and quilting
supplies (mail order and shops
across the US)*

The WARM Company
954 East Union Street, Seattle
WA 98122
Tel: 1 800 234 WARM
www.warmcompany.com
UK Distributor: W. Williams &
Sons Ltd
Tel: 017 263 7311
*For polyester filling, cotton wadding
(batting) and Steam-A-Seam 2
fusible web*

Acknowledgments

My very special thanks go to all the girls at David & Charles, especially Jane Trollope who was able to see that my enthusiastic garblings during our first telephone conversation could be turned into a book, and of course my ever-patient editor Lin, who then had to turn my enthusiastic writings and scribbles into script. To Kim Sayer for the lovely, lovely photos at a most idyllic location, The Mill, in Devon, kindly lent by Debbie Jackson – thank you Debbie.

My grateful thanks go to my lovely ladies strewn across Sussex, who sometimes groan at the enthusiastic, madcap ideas and techniques that I throw at them, who dash out and buy fabric and test all my patterns for me, and hardly raise their eyebrows when I get it wrong or change my idea mid-project – to Iris Primrose, Deanne, Shirley, Jenny, Di, Maggie, Gerry, Maggs, Ilene, Jenny, Ann, Juliet, Jo, Bev, Brenda, Jackie, Gerry, Penny and Mary – a huge, hugging thank you. To my great friends Kate, Gill and Sue – thank you for your support darlings! And Nanny Shirley for her cupcakes!

Stunning fabrics have been supplied from Gill at The Patchwork Dog and Basket and Sue's 'warehouse' at Daisy Chain Designs, Puddleducks and Pumpkin Patch. Thanks to Steamer Trading for supplying the cutlery in the picnic scene.

To the greatest joy in my life, my four most beautiful children, Abbie, Jess, Harrie and Harvey and to the most patient, kindest, long-suffering person ever, who makes me and this book possible – my husband, Phil, who is just so *gorgeous*!

About the Author

Mandy Shaw has been an enthusiastic 'maker of all thing lovely' most of her life. She has developed her own neat country style that incorporates family life and has turned her designs for her family and home into a cottage industry. Her patterns are available widely in patchwork shops, at quilt shows and on the Web. She writes regularly for *Fabrications* and *Homespun* magazines and teaches and lectures all over the country. Her fast, trendy, no-fuss approach to patchwork makes her classes fun, popular and unique.

Index